O E C D / P R O G R A M M E   O N   E D U C A T I O N A L   B U I L D I N G

Surplus space in schools

An opportunity

ORGANISATION FOR ECONOMIC CO-OPERATION AND DEVELOPMENT

The Organisation for Economic Co-operation and Development (OECD) was set up under a Convention signed in Paris on 14th December 1960, which provides that the OECD shall promote policies designed:

— to achieve the highest sustainable economic growth and employment and a rising standard of living in Member countries, while maintaining financial stability, and thus to contribute to the development of the world economy;
— to contribute to sound economic expansion in Member as well as non-member countries in the process of economic development;
— to contribute to the expansion of world trade on a multilateral non-discriminatory basis in accordance with international obligations.

The Members of OECD are Australia, Austria, Belgium, Canada, Denmark, Finland, France, the Federal Republic of Germany, Greece, Iceland, Ireland, Italy, Japan, Luxembourg, the Netherlands, New Zealand, Norway, Portugal, Spain, Sweden, Switzerland, Turkey, the United Kingdom and the United States. The Socialist Federal Republic of Yugoslavia is associated in certain work of the OECD, particularly that of the Programme on Educational Building.

The Programme on Educational Building (PEB) was established by the Council of the Organisation for Economic Co-operation and Development as from January 1972. Its present mandate expires at the end of 1987

The main objectives of the Programme are:

— to facilitate the exchange of information and experience on aspects of educational building judged to be important by participating Member countries;
— to promote co-operation between such Member countries regarding the technical bases for improving the quality, speed and cost effectiveness of school construction.

The Programme functions within the Directorate for Social Affairs, Manpower and Education of the Organisation in accordance with the decisions of the Council of the Organisation, under the authority of the Secretary-General. It is directed by a Steering Committee of senior government officials, and financed by participating governments.

THE OPINIONS EXPRESSED AND ARGUMENTS EMPLOYED IN THIS PUBLICATION ARE THE RESPONSIBILITY OF THE AUTHORS AND DO NOT NECESSARILY REPRESENT THOSE OF THE OECD

Publié en français sous le titre :

QUEL AVENIR
POUR LE PATRIMOINE SCOLAIRE?

Also available

SCHOOL FURNITURE by David Medd (October 1981)
(95 81 01 1) ISBN 92-64-12222-2   174 pages   £5.60   US$12.50   F56.00

BUILDING FOR SCHOOL AND COMMUNITY:

Volume I – Policies and Strategies (August 1978)
(95 78 01 1) ISBN 92-64-11784-9   212 pages   £4.90   US$10.00   F40.00

Volume II – France (June 1978)
(95 77 01 1) ISBN 92-64-11725-3   202 pages   £4.90   US$10.00   F40.00

Volume III – United States (January 1979)
(95 78 02 1) ISBN 92-64-11859-4   208 pages   £5.60   US$11.50   F46.00

Volume IV – England, Australia (February 1980)
(95 80 01 1) ISBN 92-64-12024-6   190 pages   £5.00   US$11.50   F46.00

Volume V – Sweden (March 1980)
(95 80 02 1) ISBN 92-64-12025-4   172 pages   £4.70   US$10.50   F42.00

Prices charged at the OECD Publications Office.

*THE OECD CATALOGUE OF PUBLICATIONS and supplements will be sent free of charge
on request addressed either to OECD Publications Office,
2, rue André-Pascal, 75775 PARIS CEDEX 16, or to the OECD Sales Agent in your country.*

CONTENTS

Part Six

SUMMARY OF CONCLUSIONS

CASE STUDIES

In the mid-seventies PEB studied the co-ordination of school and community facilities. One outcome of this study was an awareness of the emerging phenomenon of surplus school accomodation particularly in Canada and the United States. It became clear that surplus school spaces, highlighted by falling enrolments, would be an issue which would significantly affect educational building policies in the eighties.

PEB therefore commissioned architects Margrit Kennedy and Manfred Hegger to undertake a series of case studies to illustrate the causes of surplus, the problems and opportunities which follow and the implications for policy and planning. This latter aspect seemed particularly important for countries in which enrolment decline was yet to occur.

The studies, carried out during the period 1978-81, provide a wealth of examples and ideas for the reuse of surplus space in schools. But the studies, and the analysis of their implications, do more than suggest ways of reacting to the emergence of surplus school building stock. They also show how creative strategies can lead to positive opportunities for improving services in a community as well as minimising the management problems associated with surplus.

The economics of educational building policies have attracted greater attention in recent years than is given in this report (see for example PEB's paper "Towards Responsive Building Policies" published in 1984). However, the analysis of demographic and building statistics, the identification of the underlying forces which lead to surplus and the examples of reuse of school buildings in Kennedy's and Hegger's report will be of considerable value to anyone engaged in developing new approaches to educational building.

INTRODUCTION

School buildings with surplus capacity and unused accommodation are not a new phenomenon. Under-utilised or eventually empty schools have always tended to result from migratory movements which are a feature of the evolution of modern societies. Until recently surplus school capacity tended to be concentrated in rural areas. In urban areas it was considered a marginal phenomenon of rapidly growing educational resources.

This situation has changed dramatically. Surplus school accommodation can no longer be considered marginal. Studies carried out by PEB show that the phenomenon of surplus space in schools is developing on a greater scale than previously expected and at an accelerating pace. Falling enrolments affect not only old buildings but also buildings for which investments have not yet been amortized. While in many countries primary schools are the first to experience surplus space, the same phenomenon will soon reach secondary schools and further education institutions.

The reasons for surplus accommodation are manifold. In recent years, due to declining birth-rates, the long period of rapid and continuous expansion of educational resources has come to an end in most OECD countries. During that period educational building policies had to meet very considerable quantitative needs, created by the combined pressures of high birth rates, rapid urbanisation and prolongation of compulsory schooling. At the same time, new types of institutions had to be developed in order to match new educational structures and changing educational objectives and teaching methods.

These requirements usually had to be met at a high pace. For example, in the County of Hertfordhire, England, in the late fifties, every three weeks a new school building was finished and occupied, Similarly, in France towards the end of the 1960s one lower secondary school (Collège d'enseignement secondaire) for 600, 900, or 1 200 pupils was completed every day. Modest norms and unit costs, which were applied in order to meet expanding needs, today often result in high maintenance costs.

After many years of expansion, it seems difficult to adapt to a situation of zero growth or decline in population, funds and building activities for education. Planning for decline is not simply the opposite of planning for growth. It requires the development of new and different skills and above all positive attitudes toward non-growth innovative action. It presents a challenge and provides an opportunity to transcend the traditional boundaries of the educational sector and establish links with other social service sectors.

The question of how the surplus of available resources should be used and for what purpose cannot be answered by the educational sector alone. Once educational needs have been satisfied education authorities find themselves in a situation where they are able to cater for community and private needs as well. They practically act as real estate agents, who have to manage sizeable capital investments in the public interest. Educational building policies, therefore, need to be considered from different and wider viewpoints than in the recent past. Attention needs to be directed towards the management of the stock of educational buildings rather than the construction of new buildings and towards the significance of that stock in relation to the total stock of public buildings.

Yet the whole issue of surplus space may seem irrelevant to those countries which still have to face emergency situations and overcome a serious shortage of school buildings. For others again, the problems raised may appear to be of little relevance to the situation in some of their regions where quantitative needs are still significant. The experience of countries or regions which often have been caught unawares by the phenomenon, shows however that there is a strong possibility that surplus may occur locally even before major construction efforts are completed. It is important therefore to consider how the future development of surplus space can be prevented through better design or better location of new facilities.

Part one

ANALYSIS OF CAUSES

Analysis of Causes

While the dominant reasons for surplus school accommodation may vary from one locality to the next, six major groups of causes can be identified in all highly industrialised countries — declining birth rates; planning faults resulting from the lack of forecasting or acceptance of its results; population movements from rural to urban or from inner city to suburban areas or again, as of late, in the reverse direction; the aging cycle of the population in new housing areas; educational reorganisation; and municipal reforms, redistricting and urban renewal measures. Among these causes declining birth rates are by far the most dominant and will, therefore, be treated in more detail than the others and in relation to the difficult problem of forecasting.

Figure 1 shows the changes in school population in OECD countries between 1970 and 1975 as well as between 1975 and 1982. While some countries still show an overall increase in enrolments, the majority shows a decline. Actual and projected school population figures for France, Germany, the United Kingdom and the United States (Figure 2) indicate that declining enrolments are not a temporary problem but will exist at least for the next decade. They also show that the scope of the problem is considerable. In West Germany for example births dropped from more than 1 million in 1966 to less than 600 000 in 1976. Similar developments occur in all countries in which PEB collected information or conducted case studies for the present study — Australia, Canada, France, Germany, New Zealand, Sweden, the United Kingdom and the United States.

Whether or not an upswing in population figures is to be expected during the second half of the 1980s or early 1990s is not only a technical problem of forecasting but also a political question. Depending on their basic assumptions concerning social or individual values and economic developments which influence fertility rates, experts often answer this question in different ways.

Figure 1. Changes in School Population in OECD Countries 1970-75 and 1975-82

	PRIMARY		COMPULSORY		TOTAL SECONDARY	
	1970-1975	1975-1982	1970-1975	1975-1982	1970-1975	1975-1982
AUSTRALIA	1.3	0.2	0.3	0.4 d)	2.6	0.4
AUSTRIA	1.2	4.8	0.5	3.7	2.8	1.0
BELGIUM	1.2	2.7			2.6	0.4
CANADA	2.2	1.0	1.3	3.5	1.1	1.5
DENMARK	2.6	1.8	2.0	0.3 / b)1.3		3.4
FINLAND	1.2	3.0	0.6	2.6	0.3	0.4
FRANCE	0.7	0.7	0.4	0.7	1.9	0.7
GERMANY	1.2	6.8	2.1	5.8	4.9	0.3
GREECE	0.2	0.5	0.2	7.6 d)	5.0	1.8 d)
ICELAND	0.1	0.8	0.1	1.6	1.5	0.4
IRELAND	0.8 a)	0.6	1.9 b)	0.7	5.3 a)	1.9
ITALIE	0.1	1.9	1.6	1.0	4.8	1.3
JAPAN	1.5 a)	2.0	1.1 a)	2.1	0.2 a)	2.1
LUXEMBOURG	0.5	3.7	c)1.5	1.4	a) 0.2	1.0
NETHERLANDS	0.1	2.7	3.7	1.4	4.7	1.7
NEW ZEALAND	0.3	1.3	0.9	8.2	2.9	0.1
NORWAY	0.1	0.7	0.7	0.4 e)	2.0	2.0 e)
PORTUGAL	0.5	0.2	1.0	0.6	8.9	0.5
SPAIN	2.2	0.1	1.5	0.2	9.5	3.9
SWEDEN	2.1 a)	0.9	1.3 a)	0.1	a) 0.8	2.6
SWITZERLAND	4.1		1.6			2.7
TURKEY	2.0	1.5	2.0 b)	4.8	5.0 b)	
UNITED KINGDOM	0.0	3.5	3.2	e)2.4	4.8	0.5 e)
UNITED STATES	2.2	4.0	1.0	5.2	1.0	0.6
YUGOSLAVIA	1.1	0.5	0.4 b)	0.4		0.8

a) 1970-74
b) 1970-73
c) 1970-72
d) 1975-80
e) 1975-80

Source: OECD Educational Data File.

12

Figure 2. **Actual and Projected School Population in England and Wales, France, Germany and the United States**

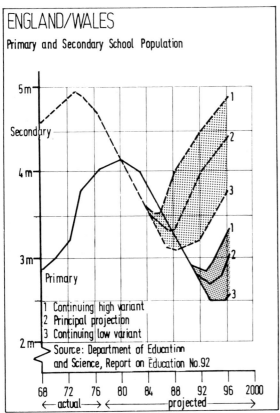

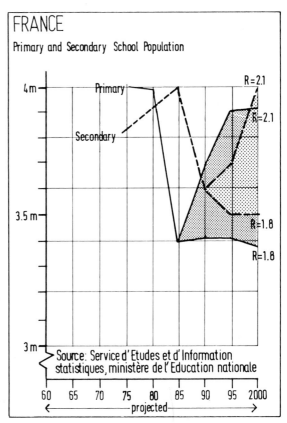

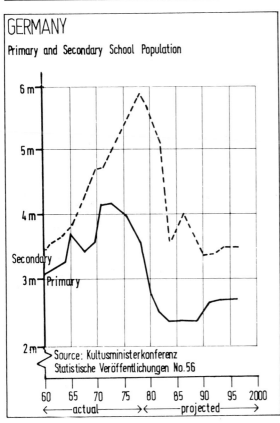

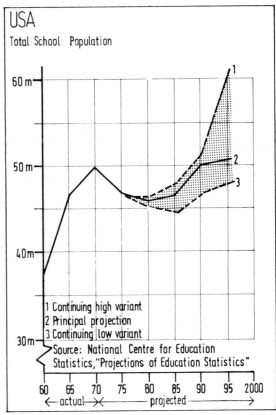

The discussion of different assumptions and their accuracy in terms of recent population figures has been particularly explicit in Ontario, Canada. Here, the Commission on Declining Enrolments deals in its Final Report[1] with three sets of projections on births, school populations and/or enrolments in their province. The three sets each contain multiple projections using different assumptions about fertility and about net migration.

Figure 3 *a)* gives the number of live births for Ontario in the most recent projections prepared by Statistics Canada, for the period 1976-77 to 2001-02. Figure 3 *b)* gives the number of live

Figure 3. **Actual and Projected Live Births for Ontario, Canada, 1921 to 2001**

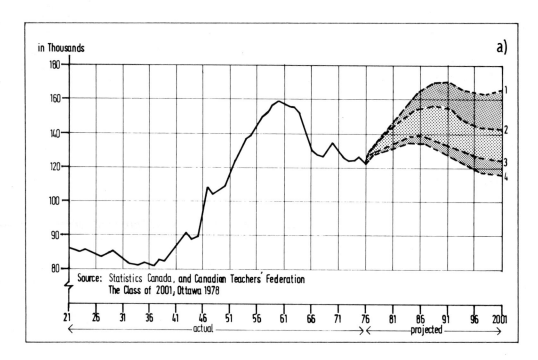

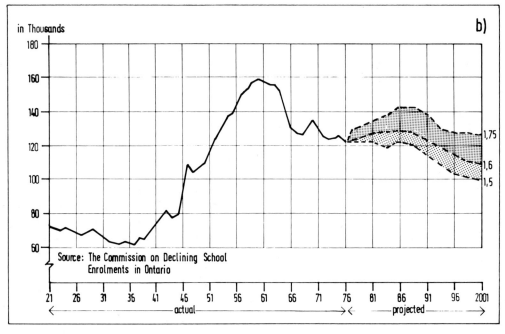

births projected to the end of this century for three of the nine projections prepared by the Commission. Although these are far lower than the projections prepared by Statistics Canada the continuing decline in the number of births through 1978 and the beginning of 1979 seems to indicate that even the middle curve (assumed to present the most likely forecast) may be too high. This means that the lowest curve may soon appear to be the most probable estimation of future births, and the "Echo of the Baby Boom" predicted so often and so forcefully by observers of the demographic scene in Ontario cannot be heard even faintly. Since the projections of births used by most planners, many academic demographers and virtually all education officials and spokesmen were all too high, this may well lead to a revision of educational policies, in particular in relation to use of surplus school accommodation.

While little is known about the socio-cultural determinants of fertility and birth rates — whether they will go up again with the return of more prosperous times, whether they relate to housing costs and housing shortage, or physical, pharmaceutical and surgical birth control measures — it is the births themselves, recent and future, that are of immediate relevance to the future demand for school services.

Without precise population forecasts, therefore, planning faults can hardly be avoided. Figure 4 shows the development of the school population and ensuing surplus school accommodation in a new housing area of a medium-sized town in France. Here, the high number of surplus classrooms resulted from the strict application of current national norms for the provision of schools in new housing areas and from the lack of mechanisms to adjust these to the local situation.

Precise forecasts cannot alone guarantee the avoidance of planning faults. This is shown by two further examples. Both in Etobicoke, Ontario, Canada and Sollefteå, a rural area in the north of Sweden (see Case Studies), forecasts of population decline and their implications for the educational system were known years before the actual surplus of school accommodation became evident. In the first example highly sophisticated forecasts came from the Ontario Institute for Studies in Education. In the second example it was "only" the local school director who had gathered enough data to show the decline in population and its impact on the school system. In both cases, however, the forecasts had little effect at the time of their appearance on the actual decisions taken in terms of new school buildings as it was politically unfeasible to deal with decline openly. As in many other examples "decline" was equated with "sickness" which had to be hidden as long as possible because it seemed to indicate political failure to produce "growth" which was equated with a "healthy" state of affairs.

While declining birth rates and planning faults based on the non-existence of or non-adherence to population forecasts are two main reasons for the occurrence of surplus accommodation in many countries, a number of other demographic and social factors tend to affect the scope of the surplus at the local level. A third group of factors relates to population movements from rural to urban or from inner city to suburban areas in all highly industrialised countries. They may be a result of changes in the industrial sector and employment patterns, as well as social and environmental preferences. Often they occur in combination with a changing social or ethnic structure of the population. In Chicago, for example, the move of the white middle class to the suburbs caused an increase in the number of school children from larger, black families replacing the white inhabitants in the inner city during the 1960s and 1970s. Now with the advent of rising oil prices and increasing housing costs in the suburbs many white couples return to the inner city. Since they usually have fewer or no children the long term plans of the Chicago school system are again in the process of being changed and adjusted, often with a view to providing other than educational services in schools.

Figure 4. **Development of Surplus School Accommodation in a Housing Estate (1 300 Dwellings) in a Medium-Size Town in France**

	Number of children			Number of classes 1976-77		
	1972-73	1974-75	1976-77	Total	Occupied	Empty
Nursery						
School A	210	205	188	6	5	1
School B	87	80	73	2	2	0
Primary						
School C	201	160	120	14	4	10
School D	173	154	140	14	6	8
School E	108	97	87	6	4	2
School F	97	94	91	6	4	2
Total	876	790	699	48	25	23

Source : The Education Service of the Town.

The aging cycle of a population in new housing areas is a fourth group of factors influencing surplus school accommodation. New towns or suburban areas, for example, usually attract relatively young families with children who settle within a short period of time. After the completion of their education, the young people move out of the area, while parents stay on. Figure 5 shows the changing age structure of the population in new housing areas according to different assumptions. This changing age structure obviously implies changes in the social needs of the popula-

Figure 5. **Population Trends in New Human Settlements**

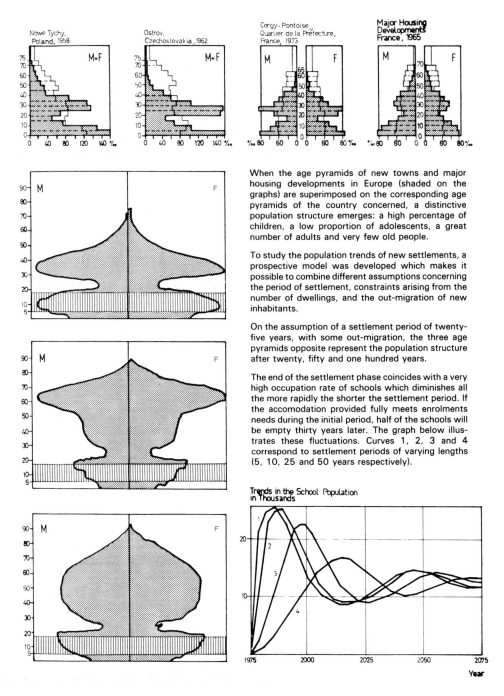

When the age pyramids of new towns and major housing developments in Europe (shaded on the graphs) are superimposed on the corresponding age pyramids of the country concerned, a distinctive population structure emerges: a high percentage of children, a low proportion of adolescents, a great number of adults and very few old people.

To study the population trends of new settlements, a prospective model was developed which makes it possible to combine different assumptions concerning the period of settlement, constraints arising from the number of dwellings, and the out-migration of new inhabitants.

On the assumption of a settlement period of twenty-five years, with some out-migration, the three age pyramids opposite represent the population structure after twenty, fifty and one hundred years.

The end of the settlement phase coincides with a very high occupation rate of schools which diminishes all the more rapidly the shorter the settlement period. If the accomodation provided fully meets enrolments needs during the initial period, half of the schools will be empty thirty years later. The graph below illustrates these fluctuations. Curves 1, 2, 3 and 4 correspond to settlement periods of varying lengths (5, 10, 25 and 50 years respectively).

Source: H. Le Bras and J.C. Chesnais, "Cycle de l'habitat et âge des habitants", *Population*, March/April 1976.

tion. If development occurs too fast, it often takes several decades before a sufficient number of young families return and a balanced heterogeneous age structure provides a stable population base for the educational sector. In addition, this process is often hampered by the rising cost of land which forces young families to move out further and allows only the more affluent social groups with few or no children to buy property in older suburban areas.

Educational reorganisation, new norms and standards, shifts in preferences for different types of schools and the physical state of school buildings are a fifth common group of educational factors causing surplus accommodation. The educational reorganisation in Ticino, Switzerland (Figure 6)

Figure 6.   Educational Reorganisation in Ticino, Switzerland

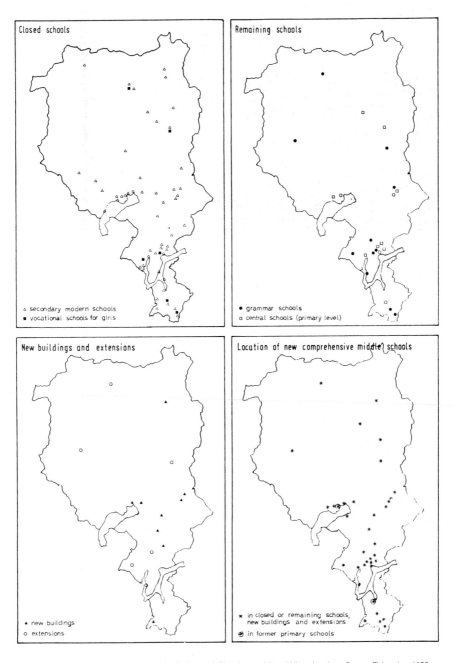

Source: Based on *Edilizia scolastica — considerazioni generali*, Dipartimento della pubblica educazione, Cantone Ticino, June 1977.

17

demonstrates the effects of the introduction of comprehensive middle schools replacing the earlier tiered system.

Municipal reforms, redistricting and urban renewal measures constitute a last group of factors frequently resulting in surplus space in schools. They are usually accompanied by a trend towards centralisation and larger administrative units providing the bases for larger schools and a surplus of older and smaller schools.

The precise extent, the quantity and distribution of surplus accommodation varies greatly from one locality to the next. Even within the same county or region overcrowding and needs for new buildings may exist side by side with surplus space. National aggregate data, therefore, are of little value for local analysis and search for solutions. However, they may help to set the local problem in a wider context and reduce the fear of being the only ones hit by the new unprecedented phenomenon of decline.

The effects on surplus obviously increase if two or more factors of decline combine. The case study of Sollefteå, Sweden, for example, shows how a combination of demographic and educational change, economic decline and municipal reform has resulted in a surplus of more than two thirds of the existing schools. A very different set of factors produced a similarly high surplus in the case of Arlington Heights, a suburban area near Chicago. Here, the aging cycle of the community — the area was built up during the 1950s and 1960s — combined with the high price of land resulted in a gross surplus of 60 per cent of all school facilities (see Case Study). Very different solutions were arrived at in these two cases.

The industrial use of surplus accommodation in the Sollefteå region, for instance, is a direct answer to its need for new employment opportunities and takes advantage of the relatively isolated location of the schools. The use of two primary schools in Arlington Heights for secondary and higher education is a direct response to the growing educational needs of a neighbouring district based on the possibilities which the relatively central location of the facilities offered.

The two examples demonstrate that an analysis of the causes for surplus accommodation is not an academic exercise as these influence the solutions which can be applied.

NOTE

1. The Commission on Declining Enrolments in Ontario, *Implication of Declining Enrolment for the Schools of Ontario: A Statement of Effects and Solutions,* Final Report, Toronto, October 1978.

Part two

ASSESSING SURPLUS AND NEEDS

Definition of Surplus

Surplus space arises from the impossibility of maintaining a permanent balance between the capacity of the building stock and actual enrolments. In many cases this may be regarded as quite normal. Only the quantity of surplus can be considered abnormal, when it exceeds the threshold beyond which no use is automatically found for it and when making use of it requires special measures. The definition of the threshold can hardly be objective and frequently varies according to the attention authorities pay to the phenomenon but also to educational, political or social objectives.

In order to clarify the notion of surplus space it was found useful in the present study to distinguish between: gross surplus, available surplus and net surplus.

— When account is taken only of the purposes which each item of the stock at present serves, accommodation which exceeds what is needed to satisfy these purposes constitutes *gross surplus.*

— When, without modifying the purposes of the present use of school buildings, an effort is made to alleviate overcrowding or to attenuate qualitative inconsistency, this leads to a reduction of gross surplus. The surplus which then remains constitutes *available surplus.*

— Available surplus can then be used to allow school buildings to serve other purposes — educational as well as non-educational — than those which they are serving at the moment. Remaining spaces constitute *net surplus.*

The terms used here do not coincide with local or national terminology. However, similar definitions have been used elsewhere to discuss surplus in its various forms.

Experience shows that it is difficult to assess the real extent of surplus accurately. While a growing number of schools are underutilised in relation to current norms, new demands are emerging for qualitative improvements in education, for more spacious accomodation and for more differentiated educational purposes. With emerging surplus space in schools the conditions, which were acceptable during an emergency period, can be improved.

Furthermore, in most cases the stock of school buildings has been accumulated over many years,

it is therefore far from consistent in quality. Buildings differ in the purposes they were built for, in the extent they have been adapted or extended to serve later purposes, and thus in their suitability for present purposes. The British *Study of School Building*[1] which is the first attempt at national stock evaluation, shows that current qualitative expectations together with needs arising from educational developments result in deficiencies in many school buildings (Figure 7). There are also great differences in their state of repair, in the quality of their service installations and their running costs. This qualitative inconsistency of the stock seems less and less acceptable in all countries studied. Therefore the real extent of surplus cannot be properly assessed without first considering how this inconsistency can be reduced.

From what precedes, it will be apparent that the notion of surplus space is always relative. The definition of capacity on which it is dependent implies reference to the quantity and quality of accommodation needed for the educational purpose to be served, i.e. on quantitative and qualitative norms. However, such norms are neither absolute nor immutable. They represent no more than the compromise reached at a given point in time between what is desirable and what is possible, given all constraints. Since such compromise and its possible modification are dependent on policy decisions, the quantity of surplus space at any given time depends largely on political priorities or policy choices.

Stock Evaluation

To provide a basis for a more informed decision-making process concerning the planning and management of educational buildings, and to facilitate their effective use by local authorities, other governmental agencies and the community at large, it is necessary to undertake an evaluation of the existing stock in order to:

— Identify deficiencies and gaps in respect of current or known future norms, educational priorities and building codes;

— Estimate what financial resources and building works will be desirable in the future, either for necessary increases in the stock, or for making good its deficiencies, or yet again for meeting running costs and for maintaining the stock in satisfactory condition;

Figure 7.   Evaluation of Secondary Schools in England and Wales, 1976

Overcrowding of Secondary Schools

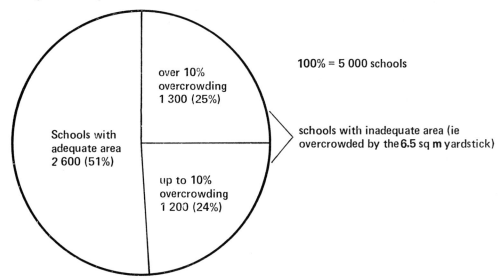

100% = 5 000 schools

over 10% overcrowding 1 300 (25%)

Schools with adequate area 2 600 (51%)

schools with inadequate area (ie overcrowded by the 6.5 sq m yardstick)

up to 10% overcrowding 1 200 (24%)

Proportions of Secondary Schools with Deficiencies in Practical Accommodation and Large Spaces

Practical Accommodation

Large Spaces

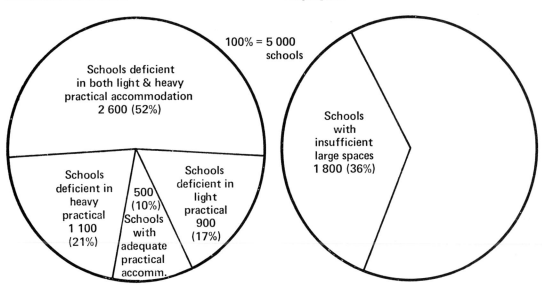

100% = 5 000 schools

Schools deficient in both light & heavy practical accommodation 2 600 (52%)

Schools deficient in heavy practical 1 100 (21%)

500 (10%) Schools with adequate practical accomm.

Schools deficient in light practical 900 (17%)

Schools with insufficient large spaces 1 800 (36%)

Proportions of pre-1946 Secondary Schools with Particular Deficiencies

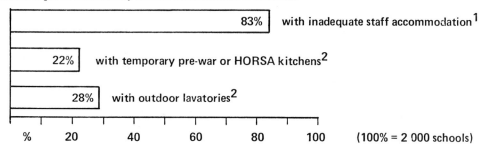

83% with inadequate staff accommodation[1]

22% with temporary pre-war or HORSA kitchens[2]

28% with outdoor lavatories[2]

%   20   40   60   80   100   (100% = 2 000 schools)

1. The yardstick has been taken as 5.5 sq m per secondary teacher.
2. Information derived from the smaller Supplementary School Building Survey.

Source: A Study of School Building, Department of Education and Science and Welsh Office, HMSO, London, 1977.

— Check to what extent buildings are consistent with, for example, socio-economic requirements and energy conservation objectives or whether they can be included in minor work programmes to counter cyclical unemployment.

In order to find practical techniques for stock evaluation, a current PEB activity is concerned with the monitoring of country experiences in this area. It is clear from the work done to date that the value of the stock of educational buildings — and that applies to surplus space as well — cannot usefully be expressed in financial terms alone. To be useful it must be assessed by a number of indicators showing:

— Total quantity expressed in floor area, work places or user capacity;

— Quantity by type of accommodation: general teaching areas, specialised areas of various kinds, etc.;

— Geographical location;

— Physical condition;

— Potential for adaptation, conversion or remodelling;

— Energy demand and other aspects of running costs;

— Social and psychological value of the facilities to the community.

Evidently, a thorough investigation covering all these points, including a continuous updating mechanism, requires special funds and skills which very few local, regional or national education authorities, so far, have considered important enough to provide. The case studies show, however, that even a crude evaluation of the existing stock may provide considerable educational, social and economic benefits. It does not necessarily depend on the sophistication of the techniques used whether the evaluation makes sense or not, but on the political will to discuss its results openly.

Today education authorities are recognizing declining enrolments and shrinking public resources as a general phenomenon and they are beginning to see the opportunities as well as the problems of this development. Often a first step consists in trying to maximize the use of existing resources by means of a more precise data base. Through an inventory of its existing stock, the municipality of Västerås, for example, found out that it had a growing overcapacity for its lower and middle levels of the nine-year compulsory school, the Grundskola, and an undercapacity for the upper level. An open discussion between the education authority and local citizens of the "balance sheet" (Figure 8) led to various new measures:

— The decision to bus children from areas with under-capacity to areas with over-capacity;

— The decision not to build four but only three schools for the lower and middle levels of the Grundskola in Önsta-Gryta, a new suburb in the northern part of the town (Figure 9);

— The consideration of alternative forms of urban planning (the phased development of new residential areas in order to achieve a more balanced and heterogeneous composition of the population);

— The development of a more adaptable type of school, a mixture of permanent core and temporary accommodation units.

Stock evaluation seems a necessary precondition to alert political representatives and members of the community before surplus school accomodation becomes a political, social and economic problem. Techniques and areas of investigation need to be chosen in the light of the existing data base, the specific purpose of the evaluation, and the manpower and money available. Purpose and scope must be carefully defined.

In this context, particular attention should be paid to recent initiatives in some countries to develop information systems or methodologies for stock evaluation for use by local authorities.

— In the United Kingdom, following the publication of *A Study of School Building*, which analyses the results of an evaluation carried out at national level, the central authorities have initiated a series of discussions with regional and local authorities with a view to ensuring continuous stock evaluation at local level [2].

— The Schulbau Institut der Länder (The School Building Institute of the German States) has published techniques and guidelines for stock evaluation intended for local authorities [3].

— The Ontario Institute of Studies in Education (OISE) has produced a computer based information system providing a wide range of data

Figure 8.   Evolution of the Lower and Middle Levels of the Grundskola (1st to 6th Year of Schooling) in Västerås, Sweden

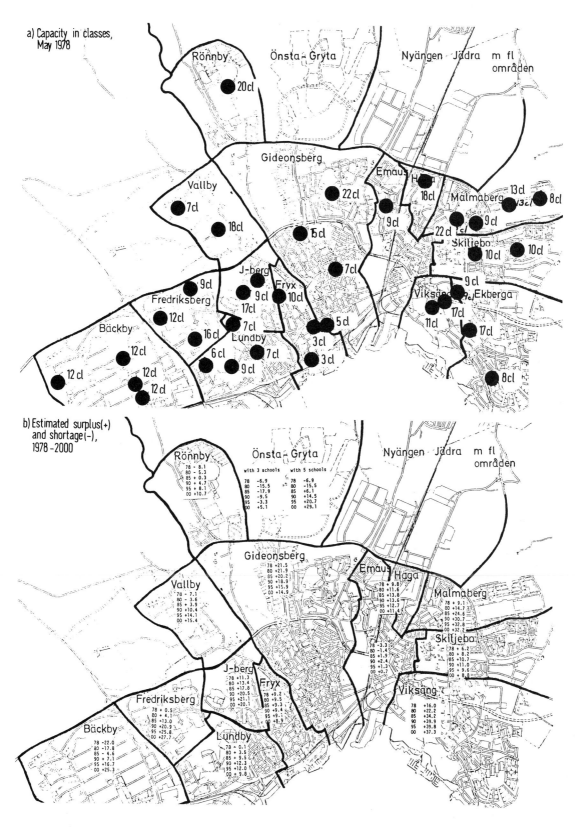

Source: "The Elementary School's Need of Premises", SU 1977:6, Statistics and Research Department, The Municipality of Västerås.

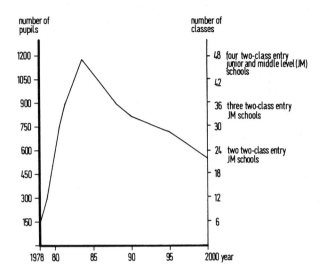

Figure 9. School Population Forecast for Önsta-Gryta, Västerås, in Relation to Number of Classes Needed at the Lower and Middle Levels of the Grundskola

Source: "Estimation of the Junior and Middle Level Needs in Önsta-Gryta", Statistics and Research Department, The Municipality of Västerås.

for use by districts and municipalities and including a feedback arrangement[4].

— In Sweden, information on the evaluation of needs, model developed by the municipality of Västerås, is being disseminated to all local authorities by the Swedish Association of Municipalities[5].

Whatever the situation, it is important to develop an inventory system as early as possible. Essential points to consider at the outset are how the system can be updated at regular intervals and how the information about changes in the stock will be made available. Stock evaluation, thus, becomes a process which is essential for meeting present as well as future needs of the educational system.

Assessment of Needs

The fact that the determination of surplus is always a matter of policy choice becomes particularly clear in the attempt to assess the needs for space. The central questions which immediately arise are: whose needs are to be taken into account and in what order?

While it seems natural to assume that educational needs will be considered first, the range of what is to be considered under "educational needs" may already be perplexing:

— Does it include only the needs of the educational district in which surplus occurs or does it also include the needs of a neighbouring school district or region?

— Does it pertain to the needs of one level of education only, e.g. compulsory education, or to those of all levels, including higher and recurrent education?

— Does school education come prior to adult or community education in all its different forms, or is the neglected field of special and rehabilitative education a first priority?

These questions are becoming a major concern to school districts which often lack the staff, skill, or political legitimacy to deal with them.

The assessment of community needs raises similar problems and may open even wider possibilities for reuse. The report prepared for the Grampian Region on "Roll Forecasting and Rationalisation of Accomodation" states:

" Perhaps the greatest problem was encountered not in the physical appraisal of the schools, but in the assessment of the value of the existing pattern of school provision to the local communities. It was obviously essential that the value to the community of the various schools, the use made of existing facilities and the possible effect of closures and amalgamation on the community should be taken account of and the services of the Community Educational Branch of the Education Department were enlisted for this purpose"[6].

Where needs are evaluated in response to the availability of space, this assessment is often limited in its purpose, i.e. it is usually not an all-encompassing survey of community needs but rather an analysis of what needs may be covered in a specific case. A comprehensive approach may take too much time and resources. A purely ad hoc approach may result in favouring the most powerful groups only. A balanced approach between these two extremes seems to produce more satisfactory results. In Cologne, for instance, decentralised social service agencies and monitoring groups gather information and data about social needs of all sectors of the community. When school space becomes available, established needs can be satisfied immediately.

24

One of the first steps in the assessment of needs will be the study of population figures and forecasts and of economic and other factors influencing population movements. In this context general population figures are of little value as they do not reflect shifts by age group and by locality. Even local population forecasts may be of limited value since they often concern compulsory attendance programmes only. The most pertinent needs are often derived from more specific sources and local preferences. They must therefore be assessed locally.

One important question in decision-making is whether the surplus is temporary or not. If the accommodation is likely to be needed again in the future to meet educational needs, the assessment will have to be directed towards finding temporary uses for it over an interim period. The case study of Sollefteå shows that the insecurity about new developments (housing, industry, etc.) may lead the education authority to hold on to its real estate assets for as long as possible and to choose the temporary user very carefully to allow for possible future changes in its own needs.

To be successful the assessment of needs demands contacts with all groups concerned within the community, i.e. parents, pupils, staff, clubs and associations. No education authority should be regarded as being competent to decide on these matters in isolation. The school system is part of the community, not an agency with complete operational autonomy[7]. In Ontario, Canada, for example school accommodation which is surplus has to be offered first to other school boards, second to universities, third to the municipality. Only if all three reject to buy or lease the building can it be sold in a public auction. This, however, happens less now that community groups are beginning to discover the usefulness of surplus school accommodation for their own purposes.

Timing is an additional factor. The assessment of needs too close to the date of proposed action is usually not adequate to secure understanding and support and to setting priorities in an appropriate way. If a school district is confident it will have surplus accommodation and this is usually known three to four years in advance (given proper enrolment forecasting techniques) advance contacts ought to be made within the community at least a year or two ahead of time. Information must be prepared and disseminated by the education authority and careful consideration be given to opinions, feelings and expressions from the public. When declining enrolments and the need for closing or redeploying facilities becomes a reality, it will then tend to be received with less abruptness.

NOTES

1. Department of Education & Science and Welsh Office of Education, *A Study of School Building,* HMSO, London, 1977.

2. *A Study of School Building, op. cit.*

3. Manfred Hegger, Doris Hegger-Luhnen, Peter Jockusch, Hans Joachim Krietsch, *Weiterverwendung bestehender Schulbauten, Eine Beispielsdokumentation,* Schriften des Schulbauinstituts der Länder, Heft 76, Berlin, 1977.

4. The Commission on Declining Enrolments in Ontario, *The Missing Pupils in the Schools of Ontario Today and Tomorrow: A Statement of Conditions, Causes and Issues,* Interim Report, Toronto, February 1978.

5. Västerås Kommun, Statistics and Research Departement, "Model for the Calculation of the Elementary School's Need of Premises", unpublished report, Vasterås, Sweden, September 1977.

6. Grampian Region (Scotland, United Kingdom), "Roll Forecasting and Rationalisation of Accommodation", unpublished report, p. 17.

7. For a more extensive discussion of strategies and methods for assessing community needs, see *Building for School and Community — Vol. I, Policies and Strategies,* OECD/PEB, Paris, 1978.

Part three

MAKING USE OF SURPLUS SPACE

This part attempts to analyse the various possibilities that exist for making use of surplus space, and the advantages and disadvantages of various solutions. It presents a typology of uses, discusses the pros and cons of the so-called "transfer principle" aiming at concentrating surplus to eliminate "half-empty" schools, describes the opportunities and limits of using surplus to raise standards of educational provision, shows the prerequisites for and benefits of community use and joint use and, finally, draws attention to the particular problems to which the disposal of net surplus gives rise. The order in which the possibilities for dealing with surplus are presented does not necessarily represent an order of priority. But it does reflect the order in which gross, available and net surplus have so far been dealt with in most countries.

Typology of Uses

The range of alternative uses for surplus school accommodation is almost unlimited. To identify the best possible use of surplus requires a clear idea of what the options for these spaces are. Therefore, it may be helpful to consider the kind of uses which were found in the course of this investigation.

The order in which these uses have been listed is not based on a quantitative analysis or preference for particular options, but moves from uses closely related to the educational sector to uses by other sectors of the community. In some cases, e.g. in Ontario, the list of priorities or reuse patterns follow a similar order, in others the frequency of a particular use depends entirely on specific economic, legal and social conditions and sometimes on personal or local priorities. In Massachusetts, for example a large number of surplus schools in inner city areas has been remodelled as senior citizens apartments because of legislation and grants favouring urban rehabilitation measures and the provision of accommodation for elderly people. In Oakpark, Michigan, various welfare agencies have moved from the city center to the suburb into surplus school accommodation as a result of the personal initiative and intervention of the Superintendent of Schools.

TYPOLOGY OF USES

Improving facilities for the existing educational programme by introducing or extending:
- Science laboratories
- Arts and music rooms
- Workshops
- Libraries
- Resource centres
- Facilities for handicapped pupils
- Special classes for immigrant children
- Dining areas
- Social areas

Reuse for complementary educational purposes:
- Field study centres
- Educational television centres
- Schools materials and learning programmes services
- Teachers centres

Reuse for for additional educational, scientific and information purposes:
- Pre-schools
- Special schools
- Alternative schools
- Vocational schools
- Polytechnics, Universities
- Adult education centres
- Advanced professional education centres
- Exhibition facilities and museums
- Arts centres
- Careers service centres

Reuse for social facilities:
- Youth clubs
- Neighbourhood associations/clubs

- Legal aid services
- Crisis aid services
- Family and child services

Reuse for health and welfare facilities:
- Facilities for the handicapped
- Clubs for the elderly
- Food programmes
- Drug release programmes
- Psycho-pedagogical programmes
- Hospitals
- Health centres

Reuse for recreational facilities:
- Workshops, arts & crafts facilities
- Restaurants/refreshment facilities
- Entertainment facilities/theatres
- Sports facilities

Reuse for residential facilities:
- Artists studio and residence
- Housing
- Homes for the elderly
- Homes for the handicapped
- Student accommodations
- Hostels
- Hotels

Reuse for administrative and commercial facilities:
- Official administration facilities
- Commercial office facilities
- Shops/markets
- Manufacturing facilities
- Garages
- Storage facilities

Reuse occurs not only for a single purpose but is very often combined. Thus, facilities for educational, scientific and information purposes are often linked with social, health and welfare or recreational facilities in order to extend the educational programme or to form community centres. Figure 10 presents examples of possible links between school and other community services,

Figure 10. Examples of Possible Links Between Schools and Other Community Services, Facilities and Activities

Primary and Secondary Schools	Other Education Services	Library and Information Services	Health, Social and Housing Services etc	Leisure Services	Private Clubs Societies etc	Commercial Services
Primary schools						
	Nursery Schools Nursery Classes Holiday Play schemes PTA fund raising and social activities Junior Youth Club	Public information Notices Mobile Library	Antenatal classes and clinics Mother and Baby clinics Creche Doctors Surgery Dental Surgery Community Centre Family Centre Family Housing	Childrens Playground Local Park Community Workshop Paddling Pool	Voluntary Play groups Junior Youth Clubs	Corner shops
Secondary schools						
Humanities	Adult courses in: Languages Literature History Philosophy etc Open University study centre	Lectures/Meetings Film shows Study and reference Museum services Archaeological services Local History collection	Health and Welfare training courses		Literary/Historical and Cultural societies Film society	Book shop Travel Agent
Science and technology	Adult courses in: Maths Science Workshop crafts Cooking Car maintenance etc	Reference materials Computer terminal Museum	Adult training centre	Allotment gardens Nature trails Nature reserves Community workshop	Scientific societies Historical societies St Johns Ambulance Association Industrial archaeology	DIY Shop Garden Centre
The Arts	Adult courses in: Drama Music Dance Visual arts	Reference material Picture collection Museum Exhibitions space	Adult day centre for the handicapped	Theatre/Hall Open Air Theatre Band stand Exhibition space	Music societies Dramatic groups Visual Arts Club Photographic society	Theatre Cinema Art Shop Music/Record shop
Library and Resources Centre	Reference and study Home-work Research	Lending and reference library Record and tape library Reprographic service	Health, welfare and social service information Housing information	Outdoor seating Sheltered study areas	Local news-sheet	Book shop Newsagent Stationers Public telephones Post Office Bank
Physical Education	Adult courses in: Physical education Sports Keep fit Youth Clubs Primary School swimming	Training films cctv	Courses for the physically handicapped	Indoor Sports/Recreation Outdoor Sports/Recreation Parks Adventure Playgrounds Sailing Fishing Boating	Sports clubs Ramblers/walking clubs Boating/Fishing clubs	Dance hall Bowling Alley Sauna Squash Sports shop Betting shop
Eating and Drinking	Coffee, snacks, meals		Meals on Wheels Luncheon clubs	Coffee/snack bars Licensed Bars Public Lavatories	Weddings Parties Dinners	Restaurant Cafe Take-away Banquet suite Pub
General social, communal and pastoral activities	Youth clubs PTA activities Career guidance School medical service Community Service Residential accommodation Conferences and courses Holiday play schemes	Public information Toy library	Community Centres Day centres for elderly and handicapped Housing office Employment Service Probationary service Local police service Health/Medical Centre Dental/Medical group practice Day Nursery Creche Family Housing 1 and 2 person housing	Public parks and open spaces	Housing association Community action groups Advice and guidance groups Citizens Advice Bureau Youth Clubs Political organisations Churches Ecumenical centres Meetings Bazaars Shows Exhibitions	Night Club Disco Estate Agent Employment Agent Professional Offices

Source : "School and Community", *Tha Architects Journal 26 May 1976,* reproduced in *Design Note 14,* Department of Education and Science, Architects and Building Branch, London.

facilities and activities as proposed by the English Department of Education and Science. In reusing sections of a school building, the activities to be accommodated need to be chosen carefully so that they harmonize with those of the school and enrich the educational programme.

A further point for consideration in seeking combinations of reuse is the catchment areas which schools and other social facilities, whether in public or private ownership, serve. By studying the catchment areas of existing facilities, gaps can be identified which facilitates choosing the most appropriate type of reuse[1].

Concentrating Surplus by the "Transfer Principle"

One means of reducing gross surplus in under-utilised schools is to transfer pupils from one school to another. If in the same area there are two partially empty schools, it may be possible to operate a transfer in such a way that one is empty and the other full. In practice, this "transfer principle" is often applied to a group of schools. A larger number of schools makes this principle easier to operate. It aims primarily at ensuring that no school's enrolment falls below a certain threshold, which is considered viable educationally or with respect to the best use of resources — including teachers — or in terms of maintenance costs (see Case Study of Arlington Heights).

The application of this principle often results in empty schools, which are closed and handed over to other uses, sold or mothballed. This may be acceptable in some instances, in most cases it is a serious problem because parents do not particularly want to send their children to schools in other neighbourhoods when there is a school in the middle of their own neighbourhood.

In small villages, local schools may form an essential part of village life. "Take away the school what remains? Nothing!" was the reaction of a mayor in a rural area in France, where a sizeable proportion of primary schools have been closed between 1962 and 1976 (Figure 11). In most cases the population did not decline in absolute terms but in terms of children gradually replaced by an aging population. The villages in which schools have been closed are often the smallest (between 100 and 500 inhabitants). Here, the school, together with the post office and the

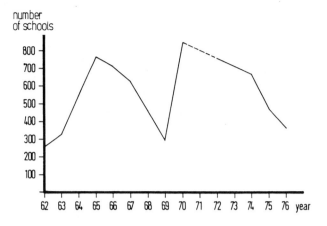

Figure 11. **Number of Primary Schools Closed in France between 1962 and 1976**

Source: Service d'Études et d'Information statistiques, ministère de l'Éducation nationale.

grocer is a symbol of vitality, the disappearance of which signals decay. This is why, regularly, even if closures occur less frequently today, the first indications of school closing give rise to strong reactions in the local press.

Despite its advantages, a policy based on the transfer principle is therefore open to serious objections. First is the risk of depriving the community of an important element in local life and increasing the difficulties involved in transporting pupils. Those responsible for decisions on school closures are well aware of these disadvantages. But there are other, perhaps less obvious, objections. The closure of a school may contribute to aggravating the economic and demographic difficulties which led to it or even making them irreversible. It also acts counter to current attitudes of the public who increasingly recognizes the intrinsic value of the existing built environment, the importance of social facilities to the community and the symbolic value of school buildings. Finally, school closures are often accompanied by an over-concentration of the school network, resulting in large schools. This trend ignores the growing preference for small school units close to the neighbourhood they serve. An example of policy measures to prevent school closures and their negative effects is to be found in the region of Chinon, France. Regrouping pupils by grade and arranging a transport system (distances are short) made it possible to preserve the schools in the villages concerned (Figure 12).

In addition, it is not even clear if school closures will save money in the long run. In some cases they

Figure 12. Regrouping of Pupils by Grade in the Rural Area of Chinon, France

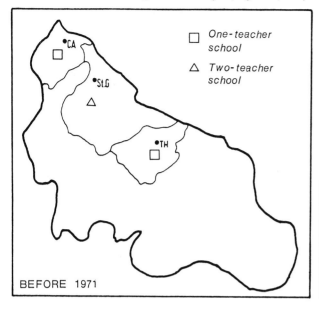

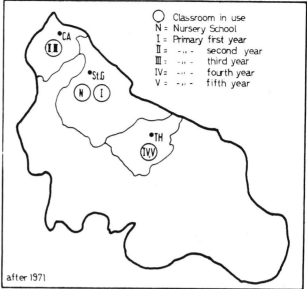

Source: Pour une politique communale de l'enfance, AGAM, Marseille, 1976.

may require extensions to existing schools to accommodate special subjects which could have been taught by "travelling teachers" (i.e. mobile teachers for specialised subjects) in smaller schools. Secondly, bussing (not for racial reasons as in the United States but for educational or economic reasons in these cases) may prove far more expensive in remote regions than in urban areas. In predominantly rural areas as in Niedersachsen in West Germany the budget spent on school transport may amount to 10 per cent of the total educational budget with pupils riding up to 100 km. daily. More important than this aspect may be the social costs which are harder to measure: bus rides represent hours of many children's lives wasted, they reduce their energy for more productive activities and they are potentially dangerous (mainly in view of the low quality of school buses in most countries).

Raising Standards of Educational Provision

Before decisions are taken to transfer pupils and close schools, many schools will operate with reduced enrolments and reduced staff. Due to the inflexibility of classrooms to shrink proportionally with enrolment decline, school buildings will be used less intensively. In many cases this is justifiable since it allows older schools to be brought up to current norms and standards. In Berslem, Staffordhire, England, for instance, all inner city schools were built in the 19th century. Surplus accommodation, here, proves to be an opportunity to reduce overcrowding and to provide needed facilities such as staff rooms and science or art rooms[2].

Even where surplus accommodation occurs in new schools built to current standards one finds improvements in working conditions. Thus, the Comprehensive School (Gesamtschule) Mümmelmannsberg in Hamburg which was first occupied in 1975 now uses surplus accommodation to install social areas equipped by pupils and teachers (Figure 13).

Four infant and nursery schools in Nottingham, England, are housed in parts of underutilised primary schools. The provision made includes a kitchen and a small community lounge for staff and parents (Figure 14). This small non-standard addition has helped considerably to improve the relationship between school and parents.

Surplus primary school space (lower and middle levels) has been used to accommodate a new teacher training college for nursery school teachers in Västerås. The school was constructed in 1915

(Figure 15) and it has been remodelled with considerable effort and care for its new use.

Special education and rehabilitation programmes seem to be getting a better chance where surplus accommodation occurs. Several examples show how adaptable school spaces prove to be for a great variety of activities and programmes — often without substantial remodelling costs. A new coat of paint, the use of graphic arts, a rearrangement of furniture, sometimes curtains or carpets may be all that is needed to transform a standard class-room into a special activity area. Even where ramps and special toilets for the physically handi-capped are needed a single storey school building will prove to be easily adapted to such changes. Thus for some of the neglected pupil groups (those with physical and mental disabilities as well as those without jobs and in need of vocational training or retraining) surplus accommodation has considerably improved educational choices. In Welwyn Garden City, England, for instance, a group of multiple handicapped children had a first chance to leave hospital by being day-released to an empty primary school (Figure 16).

Improving and diversifying educational provision are becoming more and more "legitimate" ways of reducing surplus and implementing innovative educational ideas. (In contrast to the 1960s when educational innovation usually meant building anew.) The establishment of field study centres and teachers' centres are two frenquently found examples in rural and urban areas. One local authority in Wales, remodelled more than 150 vil-lage schools as outdoor education centres for pupils from outside the area (see Case Study). Similar cases of village schools are very frequent in France. There is a long tradition in this country of letting pupils from urban areas attend residential courses during the school year in the mountains ("classes de neige"), in the countryside ("classes vertes") or by the sea ("classes de mer"). Teach-ers' centres encourage teachers to contribute to their own development and to the development of schools and colleges. The Case Studies of Elm Bank Teachers' Centre in Coventry, England, and Llangefni Teachers' Centre in Wales provide exam-ples of well-equipped urban and rural centres, the latter promoting a more informal, self-help approach among teachers. In London two inner

Figure 14.   Nursery School Using Surplus Primary School Accommodation, Carlton Netherlfield Infant School, Nottingham, England

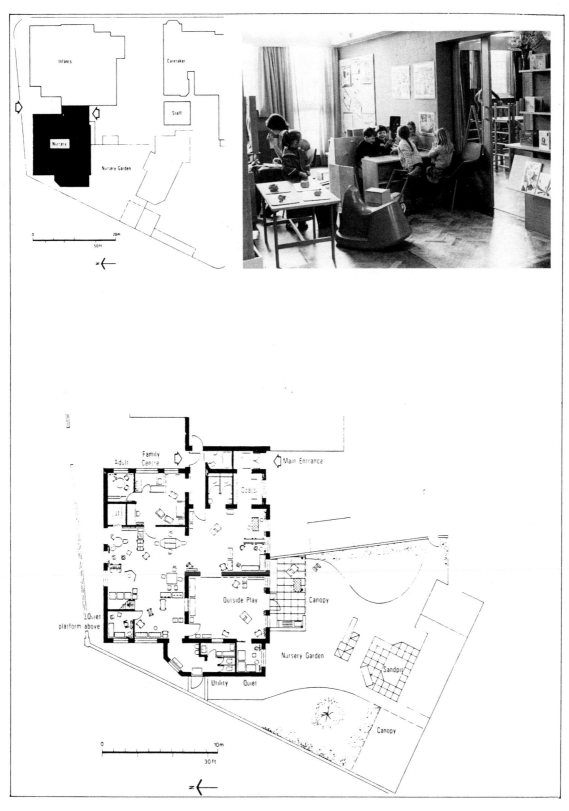

Source: "Nursery Education: Low Cost Adaptation of Spare Space in Primary Schools", *Broadsheet 1*, Department of Education and Science, Architects and Building Branch, May 1980.

Figure 15.   Primary School Converted into a Teacher Training College in Västerås, Sweden

Figure 16.   Special Education and Rehabilitation Programmes Using Surplus School Accommodation

Classroom and extension serving as gardening area for mentally handicapped children in Livonia, Michigan

Classroom transformed into dining area in the same school

Remodelled classroom used for the care of severely handicapped children, Welwyn garden City

Play area in former multi-purpose hall of the same school

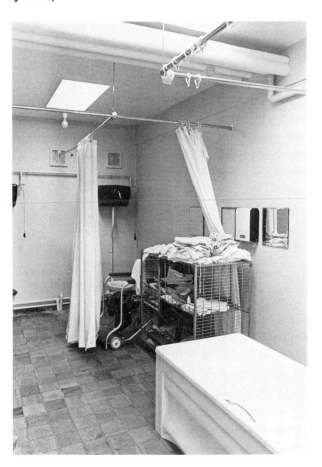 

city schools are being used as learning materials centres. One of them produces and provides cable TV programmes for Inner-London schools while the other develops and provides learning materials in audio-visual and printed form (see Case Study).

Placing Surplus at the Disposal of the Community

The discussion of the kind of educational needs which may be satisfied by surplus school accommodation sometimes hides the fact that there may be more pressing needs which stem from other public and community sectors. In fact, very few societal sectors have received as much attention and support as education over the last ten to fifteeen years. Using surplus school accommodation for other than educational purposes, therefore, may contribute to satisfying latent or expressed social needs enabling for example the creation of a medical centre, social meeting places, a youth club or a club for the elderly, which from the standpoint of the community may be more desirable than the satisfaction of additional educational needs.

In Sollefteå, Sweden, recreation centres, social centres and church assembly rooms have been accommodated in vacant school rooms (in wooden buildings) thus increasing the quantity and quality of social services for the rural population. Conversely, school buildings built with bricks and concrete have generally been given over for a relatively low (rent or sales) price to industrial or commercial uses in order to improve the employment situation (see Case Study). In Karlshafen, Germany, a group of handicapped people found virtually by accident an empty primary school in a beautiful countryside setting and successfully applied to the authorities for funds in order to redeploy this facility as a rural holiday, leisure and education centre for members of the group (Figure 17). A local independent youth club in Cologne, Germany, took over a hundred year old school building and remodelled it through self-help mainly by a group of unemployed young people (Figure 18). Apartments for the elderly have been created by a commercial developer in an old inner city school in Boston, Massachusetts (Figure 19).

The force with which such demands are expressed and the form they take, however, depend on the

Figure 17. **Primary School Converted into Rural Holiday, Leisure and Education Centre for Handicapped Adults in Karlshafen, Germany**

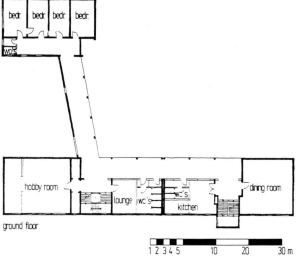

Source: Drawing by the authors.

extent to which public agencies, voluntary groups or associations requiring accommodation for their activities are aware of the opportunities offered. When these activities relate to educational activities, there may be a possibility for joint or shared use of educational buildings. When, on the other hand, the activities of the community sector are perceived as requiring exclusive use of facilities, competition may arise between these needs and those of the educational sector or other public sectors.

The choice rarely presents itself in terms of simple alternatives but more often in terms of setting priorities between various ways of using the resources represented by the surplus itself and the complementary funds needed for its reuse. Such decisions no longer depend on educational building policies alone. They imply that such policies, in one way or another, take into account the building and staffing policies of other sectors. They depend, as the work of PEB on Facilities Co-ordination has shown[3], on the attitudes of the education authorities — but also of the community as a whole —

Figure 18.   Old School, Classified as a Historic building, Taken over and Managed by a Youth Club; Converted through Self-help

Figure 19.   Bowdoin School, Boston, Built in 1896, Converted into 35 Flats for the Elderly

towards the opening up of the school, the joint use of facilities and inter-service co-operation.

Where schools have been financed solely by local tax-payers, as for instance in the United States, the question of what public, semi-public or private use will serve the community best may be left to the local decision-makers (whether they are the school board, the municipality or a joint group of representatives). In other countries, mainly where joint financing (e.g. between local communities and State agencies) is the rule, the question of equity arises in relation to use of surplus space. While in principle the State may agree that community use of surplus school accommodation is a good idea, it is also clear that this may produce inequity between various localities, since quantity and quality of community facilities will vary from one area to another.

The "danger" of having to repay State investments if surplus space is occupied by other community groups may well lead to an under-utilisation, i.e. inefficient use of public assets. The Case Study of Ontario shows clearly the difficulties which arise in this context. The recommendation of the Commission on Declining School Enrolments stresses both maximum utility of the assets school facilities represent *and* the constraints associated with the requirements of equity. What this double recommendation amounts to is an attempt to create a balance between communities with surplus and those without by drawing revenues in proportion to the market value from the sale or lease of surplus school property. However, the experience of most local school boards (see also Case Study of Arlington Heights) defies such intentions. A realistic assessment of what community groups, in particular those who represent the weakest strata of society, can pay usually demonstrates clearly a widening gap between the desirability of reuse and the ability of groups to pay an adequate rent.

Experience shows that schools in rural as well as urban situations play a vital role in the life of the community outside school hours. With the advent of surplus school accommodation during school hours, this role may be considerably extended and diversified. By serving mothers, children and the elderly in the immediate neighbourhood such accommodation can be used to provide a base and meeting place for people who are at home during the day, and might become friendly "route-stops" for local shoppers. By catering for specialised activities and adding to the range of opportunities in a town centre, such facilities, because they are easily accessible by both public and private transport, could also be expected to attract users from beyond the immediate locality.

In many cases local communities, municipalities, public, semi-public and private agencies and groups have raised funds specifically to add community facilities and staff to an otherwise basic school provision. In Oakpark, Michigan, for example, a dental care centre and health museum (Figure 20) has been established in surplus primary school accommodation through donations from a regional university and parents. The centre now serves the entire region for health instruction and examinations. In Scotland, surplus accommodation in rural schools has been used to provide halls and kitchen/serveries financed by the local community. In Toronto, Ontario, "Parallel Use Committees" have been established to develop the use of surplus space. Similar endeavours to involve the community and promote active collaboration with the authorities can be found in a growing number of cases.

Dealing with net Surplus

In most countries a certain number of schools will have to be closed also in the future. Before this happens it is essential to ensure that all other possibilities have been explored, that measures

Figure 20.   Dental Care Centre and Health Museum in Former Primary School, Oakpark, Michigan

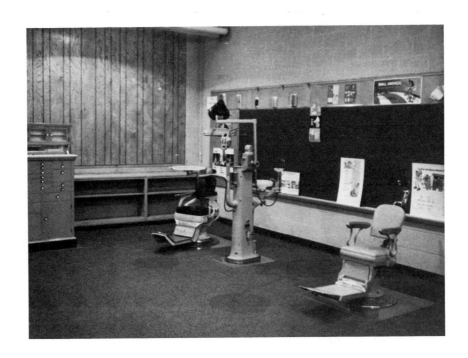

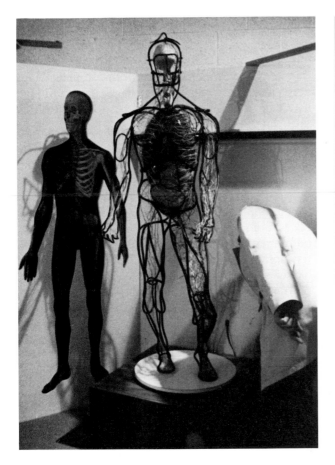

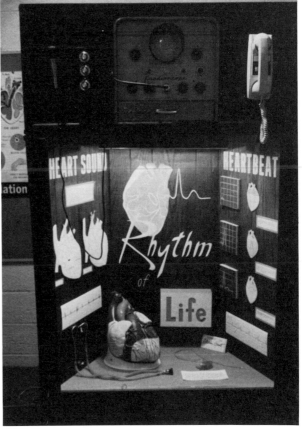

are taken to minimise the consequences and, above all, that solutions for reusing the accommodation have been planned or at least envisaged. In most instances, closing a school is a last resort, acceptable only if there are no other means of using it as a resource.

Any decision to close implies difficult choices: among a group of schools for example which ones should be closed and which communities should suffer the consequences? Furthermore, which is the margin needed to provide the necessary flexibility within a network of schools? Can a reserve not be kept in underutilised schools as well as in completely empty schools?

When the fall in enrolments is expected to be more than a temporary phenomenon, it may be useful to put some buildings in reserve thereby keeping a margin of resources to meet future fluctuations in demand. But the hypothetical advantages of this solution must be weighed against a number of disadvantages: a building which is kept temporarily out of use is exposed to the risk of vandalism and, if it is not to deteriorate, some expenditure will be needed on maintenance and heating. Boarding up windows for security purposes may also be regarded as a billboard telling the public that their investment is unused, it becomes a symbol of decline (Figure 21).

The economics of mothballing are far from simple: savings in teacher salaries and running costs may be offset to some extent by increased transportation costs, by the need for minimum maintenance, and making good damage by vandals. Letting a school stand empty usually stimulates all sorts of negative responses. In England, a Wiltshire study revealed a high correlation between village vandalism and villages without schools. In addition to problems of vandalism indirect costs may include unwanted drifts of population and a disincentive for young people to move into the area. This in turn may result in a disincentive for small industries to locate in the area thus creating a vicious circle of unemployment and out-migration.

Figure 21. **Unused and Boarded-up School, a Symbol of Decline**

As a consequence, mothballing generally is not worthwhile if there is an alternative use within the local community or if a school can be sold or, even better, let for a good price. School buildings and their sites — particularly in inner urban areas — usually represent a considerable value. The gain made from such sales in some instances might be equivalent to the cost of replacing or substantially remodelling a school elsewhere. In some cases it may be justifiable to transfer ownership or to let the school for less than the appraised value if the new use is of specific benefit to the community.

The closure of temporary accommodation is quite a different matter. *A Study of School Building*, for instance, demonstrates the inadequacies of much of the twenty-five to thirty-year old temporary accommodation units. A 1976 survey indicates that temporary buildings are on the average 40 per cent more expensive in recurrent costs than permanent buildings (Figure 22). The closure of temporary buildings, therefore, would result in higher savings than the total or partial closure of permanent school buildings[4].

Figure 22. **Economies in Recurrent Costs per Year per Place Closed in Temporary and Permanent School Buildings, England and Wales**

| | £ per place closed at 1976 survey prices[1] | |
	Permanent	Temporary
Primary		
1. Buildings related		
a) Fuel and light	5	25
b) Other	35	35
2. Fixed element (school secretaries and other ancillary staff)	5	—
3. Sub-total	45	65
4. *Less* Allowance for increased school transport costs[2]	−20	—
5. Total	£25	£65
Secondary		
1. Buildings related		
a) Fuel and light	10	45
b) Other	60	65
2. Fixed element (school secretaries and other ancillary staff)	10	—
3. Sub-total	80	110
4. *Less* Allowance for increased school transport costs[2]	−15	—
5. Total	£65	£110

1. The figures in this Table derive from the 1974/75 out-turn, re-priced to 1976 Survey prices.
2. In the absence of evidence from practical studies the estimates of the effects of closure on school transport costs should be regarded as essentially illustrative.
Note : This table is essentially illustrative and figures are rounded to the nearest £5.
Source : A *Study of School Building,* Department of Education and Science and Welsh Office, HMSO, London, 1977.

NOTES

1. "Tasks and Mechanisms", *Building for School and Community — Vol. I, Policies and Strategies, op. cit.*

2. "The Renewal of Primary Schools", in *Building Bulletin 57,* HMSO, London, 1980.

3. *Building for School and Community — Vol. I-V,* OECD/PEB, Paris, 1978-1979.

4. *A Study of School Building, op. cit.,* pp. 151-153.

Part four

MANAGEMENT OF SURPLUS

The kind of decisions which use of surplus school accommodation demands are very different from those related to the provision of new building. Only to a lesser degree can they rely on precedent as a guide and such precedents as exist are in most cases but isolated ventures. There is as yet no precedent that could serve as a basis for more comprehensive policies for the effective management of surplus. Compared to the previous period of rapid expansion, the objectives today are far more difficult to define and wider number of variables — economic, social, political — have to be taken into account. Far more partners are now involved or concerned, the diversity of the needs to be considered as well as the growing diversity of local situations directly influence choices and priorities.

The following examples illustrate this diversity.

— The Ontario Case Study shows a preoccupation with *economic problems.* In its Final Report the Commission on Declining School Enrolments in Ontario puts the emphasis on financial issues, proposing cuts in expenditure almost proportional to the reduction in student numbers[1].

— In the United States the great variety of approaches due essentially to the autonomy of local school boards, makes it impossible to distinguish any particular bias. However, the availability of *funds for special programmes,* e.g. community education, vocational training, provision for the handicapped or housing for the elderly, has often determined the way in which surplus accommmodation has been used.

— The Report of the Grampian Region in Scotland[2] as well as studies in the United Kingdom[3] and the Netherlands[4] reflect a more *social bias.* They stress the importance of the school to community life and the possibilities surplus school accommodation represents for improving social services.

Despite the diversity in the objectives and solutions adopted, it is possible to identify a number of issues, common to all situations, which greatly affect the efficient management of surplus. These can be grouped into two main questions: how and by whom are decisions taken regarding the use of surplus space, and what are the main obstacles or constraints hampering such decisions?

Participants and Modes of Co-operation

The preceding analysis of possible uses has shown clearly that the extent to which the educational sector alone can provide the answers is limited. Who then are the other partners and what are the various mechanisms whereby co-operation between them and the educational sector can be established?

In most cases, given the role of the public sector in providing the community with the services it needs or demands, the main partners are represented by the other social service sectors. The studies undertaken by PEB on Facilities Co-ordination[5] have shown the importance of inter-sectoral co-operation. The emergence of surplus space in schools at a time when shortage of resources will not allow much new facilities to be built, further demonstrates the need for such co-operation and for making it a permanent feature. It represents a means of using surplus in one sector to compensate deficits in another.

Inter-sectoral co-operation no doubt has a role to play at central level in the co-ordination of regulations, financing procedures, norms, etc., but it is at the local level that operational decisions regarding the use or reuse of educational and other social facilities are most effectively made. It is consequently at this level that the various services, each responsible for a given sector — be it education, child care, libraries, other cultural activities, health, provision for the elderly, sports, etc., — will need to get together and create such co-operation mechanisms as may best suit local circumstances. If the local district or municipality is too small, such co-ordination mechanisms may have to be conceived to ensure co-operation over district boundaries.

The action resulting from inter-sectoral co-operation practically always concerns needs that have been defined by the service sectors themselves. However, the possibilities surplus space offers often favour the expression of needs which have not yet been met or go beyond the strict competence of existing services. There is also a growing tendency among members of a community to consider facilities of all kinds — in the first instance schools — as public property, and to insist on being associated with decisions regarding their use. It is thus evident that management of surplus, if it is to be successful and developed on a wider scale, will increasingly need to involve also other participants in the decision-making process. These may range from semi-public social agencies to a variety of community groups and associations and would, to the extent possible, also need to include non-organised users.

Among these partners, special mention should be made of elected representatives at local level. Their role in any decisions concerning the use and management of surplus space is particularly important: as people responsible for managing the resources of the community, they have a direct interest in ensuring the optimum use of facilities; in addition, they are better placed than most to view the interests of the community globally.

Whatever mechanisms are set up, and this is one of the lessons to be learnt from experiences in, for example, Canada, Sweden and the United States, they will have to develop their own modes of co-operation with community groups, other potential users and elected representatives. Such mechanisms may take a number of forms.

There are many examples of solutions developed on the basis of *committee structures* such as the Parallel Use Committee in Toronto (see the Ontario Case Study) or the Special Advisory Committee established in Arlington Heights. Here, one member of the Committee is appointed by the superintendent of schools, another by the chief administrator in the county, and a third by both. This group interacts directly with a facilities co-ordinator and the respective schools to determine which alternative use of surplus school space would be most beneficial to the specific community served. Another example is that of Grampian Region, Scotland, where a *"pool" of local authorities* has been established to investigate the effects of declining enrolments and migration and jointly put forward proposals for the restructuring of the school network and the reuse of surplus accommodation.

An interesting case is that of Montgomery County, Maryland, United States, where the appointment of a *special facilities co-ordinator* made it possible to attract private and semi-private users and groups. These may settle temporarily or permanently in surplus school accommodation and, instead of paying a rent, accept to receive pupils who get a learning experience by participating in professional activities. Successful examples include a potter's workshop, a painter's studio and

an architectural office housed in schools. These experiences have enabled the education authority to adopt this type of "mutual benefit arrangement" as a new strategy for redeploying surplus space. This solution combines two advantages: full use is made of surplus space and the educational choices or options open to pupils are extended.

The degree of *autonomy* granted to individual schools or local education boards often seems to determine how well surplus school accommodation will be used as shown in the case of Montgomery County. Another example of this is Marion High School in Metropolitan Adelaide, South Australia, where despite a fall in enrolments from about 1 800 in 1965 to approximately 1 000 today there has in fact never been any available surplus because a use was found for it even before it occurred. The initiative for this development has been with the school itself — and its very dynamic headmaster. The backing of the community, the great number of volunteers and the financial support received from various funding agencies — at federal, State and local levels — have contributed to the success of this experience but without the autonomy enjoyed by the school and the self-help movement it has engendered this development could never have taken place[6].

The efficient management of surplus space further implies a redistribution of responsibilities and a redefinition of roles and tasks of all partners involved. First, as many of the experiences referred to in this report show, the role of the users becomes primordial. Unless headmasters, teachers, parents and pupils but also other members and groups of the community are motivated and ready to take on new responsibilities it is unlikely that the potential benefits of reuse — economic, social and educational — can be fully reaped. It is equally clear, however, that the users can play their role only if they receive the necessary backing and financial support.

It is worth noticing that at the start of the present investigation in 1977, there was a lack in most countries of even the most basic provision for exchanging information on the whole issue of surplus school accommodation. In a number of cases local politicians, officials, headmasters and teachers were greatly relieved when in the course of their discussions with the consultants in charge of the investigation they discovered that the problem of surplus was not something particular to their own locality or school but was in fact a national and international problem. In the meantime, a number of central authorities have begun to remedy this deficiency by organising conferences, workshops, public hearings; gathering and disseminating information; and undertaking research and development work.

In the United Kingdom, for example, regional conferences are organised at which local decision-makers have an opportunity to discuss common problems with each other and with representatives of the central authority, in this case the Architects and Building Branch of the Department of Education and Science. The latter also undertakes studies on issues of common interest to local authorities and is directly involved at the local level in a certain number of projects concerned with issues of reuse or declining enrolments and from which lessons can be learnt for future projects. The results of such studies and projects are subsequently published and widely disseminated. Similarly in Germany and Sweden the associations of municipalities and cities are getting increasingly involved in stock evaluation, and in disseminating information more widely.

Obstacles and Constraints

Reuse of surplus school accommodation raises a number of difficult questions to which the partners in the decision-making process will need to seek answers. Examples of such questions are:

— In the case of reuse for other than educational purposes, should ownership of the available facilities be transferred from the education sector to the new users, whether other public sectors or private users, or, conversely, should community use, in the widest sense, be considered as temporary or reversible in case there is an upturn of enrolments in the future?

— Will the right to use accommodation include the possibility of undertaking necessary adaptations?

— How will the expenses for such adaptations be shared between the owner and the new users?

The answers that can be given to these and other questions are dependent on a number of conditions — financial, legal, administrative, technical as well as human.

Financial procedures and the rigid sectoral compartmentation of sources of financing constitute the most common of obstacles. A re-evaluation of needs for capital investment based on inter-sectoral investigations seems to be a prerequisite for a more efficient re-allocation of available facility resources. In addition, a redistribution of funds is needed within capital expenditure budgets to restore the balance between the share devoted to new building and that reserved for the adaptation and renovation of the existing stock, to the benefit of the latter. Studies undertaken in the United Kingdom and covering situations in inner city, suburban and rural areas[7] show clearly that without such a shift of funds, it is practically impossible to make intelligent use of existing physical resources.

Financing of transformations and adaptations in relation to reuse of surplus space often present local authorities with almost insuperable difficulties. User services often resent financing building works in buildings which are not exclusively theirs or permanently assigned to them. In addition, the rules and procedures governing State subventions are such that it is often cheaper for a local authority to build anew than to renovate or adapt an existing perfectly sound building (often at a much lower total cost). This is, of course, an absurd situation. Similarly, the task of adapting public buildings to serve new needs is often left to local authorities or municipalities which do not always have the financial resources needed. It happens therefore that local authorities are forced to leave unused school buildings empty — with all the risks this entails — while at the same time a number of community needs remain unsatisfied. There is consequently an urgent need to reconsider the extent to which the cost of renovation should be incumbent on local authorities alone. The reluctance of central authorities to remedy the present situation is very frequent. An example is the refusal of the U.S. Congress to pass the so-called "Heinz Bill" to authorise the Secretary of Housing and Urban Development to make grants to local governments for converting closed school buildings to alternate uses[8].

Sectoral accountability for funds, whether in the form of local grants or State subsidies, represents a further constraint which makes it extremely difficult to work out appropriate solutions for joint or shared use of surplus space and many of the financial constraints which apply to co-ordination of facilities thus also apply to the reuse of available accommodation[9]. In the last part of this report, some indications will be given as to the kind of measures that need to be taken to facilitate the financing of renovation and reuse.

Laws and regulations often constitute a further obstacle. Probably because of a fairly long tradition of school closures in rural areas, most countries seem to have gone a long way in easing legal constraints and simplifying administrative procedures for closing and selling schools. Most State governments in the United States, for example, have revised their laws accordingly[10]. In the United Kingdom, the "Education Act" of 1944 (Section 13) already introduced deliberate policies to involve the public in decisions on school closures: it stipulates a legal requirement for publishing the notice fo closure, leaving two months during which the public is able to comment on the intention of closure to the Secretary of State. While this possibility was used only occasionally in the past, today in almost every case of intended closure serious objections are raised by the public with the result that this requirement has become a highly controversial issue[11]. Similarly, a recent law case in Germany shows that parents are increasingly aware of their power to prevent school closures. In this particular case, the journey to a neighbouring school was considered by the Court intolerable to *one* pupil both because of distance and for environmental reasons (the way to school was along a motorway) and the school consequently had to reopen[12].

These examples clearly show that there is, on the part of the public, a growing awareness of the value of the school to the community and of the possibilities surplus accommodation offers. Laws and regulations will therefore need to focus less on the negative aspects of school closures and more on positive measures to overcome problems of ownership and facilitate joint use.

Co-ordinated facilities projects have contributed to a greater acceptance of the concept of joint or shared use. Much still remains to be done to ease legal constraints impeding such use in ordinary, non co-ordinated schools. These constraints often stem from national rules, or rules laid down by the regional or local authorities themselves, and mostly concern the question of legal responsibilities. However, as in the case of co-ordinated projects, such obstacles are more easily overcome when the partners involved all belong to the public sector than when more unusual combinations are made such as a mixture of public and private uses (as in the case of Montgomery County, Maryland, United States). Here again, the solution probably lies in devolving authority to the local level, in defining more clearly, together with the various partners involved, the legal responsibilities of each and in making insurance arrangements that are better adapted to the new situation.

There is also a number of *physical and technical constraints* which may hinder the reuse of surplus space. Among these, those related to the physical condition and state of repair of a building can generally be removed relatively easily provided there is money. Conversely, the location and layout of a school often pose far more difficult problems for reuse. For example, in the case of neighbourhood primary schools located in relatively quiet residential areas the range of options for joint use or reuse is limited by zoning or land use requirements, traffic limitations and parking regulations. A solution that has sometimes been adopted in this case is to provide housing for the elderly, a type of reuse which complies with zoning laws for residential areas. The disadvantage is that remodelling is too substantial to allow subsequent reconversion to educational use, if and when the need arises. Also, as shown by the study carried out by the Borough of Etobicoke and the Metropolitan Toronto School Board in Ontario to examine the financial, social and physical feasibility of converting schools to senior citizens' accommodation[13], the proximity to essential services is a prerequisite which is rarely met in the case of neighbourhood schools in residential areas, a popular planning concept in the 1950s and 1960s.

Building regulations, especially those related to safety, constitute another group of constraints to which particular attention needs to be paid. It is clear, however, that regulations and norms relative to new building cannot be rigidly applied to cases of adaptation for reuse. Therefore, while ensuring basic requirements, those responsible at local level will need to be allowed a margin of flexibility in the interpretation of such regulations and norms, and the question then arises of how to define this margin.

Finally, among the obstacles to the effective reuse of surplus space are those which relate to *attitudes and skills*. By and large they are the same as those that tend to paralyse facilities co-ordination: sectorisation of responsibilities, exclusive appropriation of space, reluctance towards joint use, difficulties of defining priorities in relation to overall needs, difficulties of initiating or sustaining a dialogue with other partners or with the users. It would seem however that the whole issue of surplus space has made apparent a specific, yet more general attitude which risks to affect future facilities policies negatively.

Following the period of rapid expansion during the 1960s and early 1970s during which innovators were attracted in large numbers to the educational sector, the current decline in enrolments and resources seems to be accompanied by a diminishing interest for this sector on the part of creative and imaginative people. In her paper on "The Cost of Decline" Katherine E. Eisenberger has pointed out that today public education is once again under siege:

" However, this time there are no double volumed reports chronicling the years of exhaustive study and man-hours devoted to discovering the malaise; there are no scholarly commissions offering assistance in locating and purging the evil: and there are no heated debates over 'the one sure cure'. Public education is in danger of death by neglect; this is the cost of decline"[14].

There seems to be little glamour or recognition for those who are involved in the difficult task of adjusting to decline. Imaginative decisions are not very popular in a climate of fear and anxiety. They are, therefore, often stalled and the problems are left to solve themselves. Any enthusiasm is met with caution and social innovators simply tend to turn to other areas where they find more responsiveness or funds to implement their ideas. This attitude is not only defeatist but also unjustified as the many examples of innovative solutions described in this report show.

To do more with less is a major challenge which demands more skills than ever and approaches that are not only delicate and patient but also bold in imagination. Small, incremental, sometimes non professional, and fairly cheap solutions, although not recognised as "planning" or "design" solutions in the traditional sense, may well pave the way for innovations which are less visible but more far-reaching than in the past. For this to happen, however, a change of attitudes is needed on the part of all concerned towards a wider acceptance of existing resources as a means of satisfying social needs in the future. From isolated projects developed through the initiative and persistence of a few individuals, the time has now come to move towards more comprehensive policies for the use and management of existing resources.

NOTES

1. The Commission on Declining Enrolments in Ontario, Final Report, *op. cit.*, pp. 1-3.

2. Grampian Region, *op. cit.*

3. *A Study of School Building, op. cit.*

4. N.C.G. van Bossum and H.G.M. Wolfs, *The Old School Building: A Resource for the Community,* Information Centre for School Building, Rotterdam, November 1978.

5. *Building for School and Community, Vol. I-V, op. cit.*

6. Brigitte Bleys, *Marion High School Case Study,* Directorate of Educational Facilities, Education Department of South Australia, Adelaide, 1978.

7. *A Study of School Building. op. cit.*

8. U.S. Congress, Committee on Banking, Housing and Urban Affairs, "A Bill to authorize the Secretary of Housing and Urban Development to make grants to local governments for converting closed school buildings to efficient, alternate uses, and for other purposes". Introduced by Mr. Heinz, 95th Congress, 1st Session, S 792, February 24, 1977.

9. Cf. in particular *Building for School and Community — Vol. I, Policies and Strategies, op. cit.,* paragraphs 98-101.

10. Illinois State House of Representatives, *Public Act 80-858 to Amend Section 5-22 of the School Code of Illinois approved March 18, 1961,* Code LEP 80-4088, Springfield, Illinois, 1973.

   Michigan Department of Education, *Michigan's School Enrollment Decline: Projections and Implications.* A Report of the Michigan Department of Education Task Force, Lausing, Michigan, 1977.

   Susan Moore Johnson, *Declining Enrollments in the Massachusetts Public Schools: What it means and what to do,* Massachusetts Department of Education, Boston, 1978.

11 "Public Inquiry: Closing Schools", in *New Society,* July 5, 1979, p. 20.

12. *Oberverwaltungsgericht,* 9/78, Bremen.

13. The Commission on Declining Enrolments in Ontario, "School Facilities, the Community and Declining Enrolments" (Suggestions for Ontario Boards of Education), *Information Bulletin No. 1, Toronto, February 1978.*

14. Katherine E. Eisenberger, "Demographic Change: The Cost of Decline", paper prepared for the Forum of Educational Organisation Leaders, Washington D.C., 1979.

Part five

CONSEQUENCES FOR THE FUTURE

Among the causes for the emergence of surplus space, analysed in the first part of the report, some are of a permanent nature. Declining birth rates may not persist and do not affect all countries whereas other demographic factors will continue to cause fluctuations in enrolments and create local disparities between needs and resources. Population movements between different areas and changes in the social structure or age structure of the population within a given area are likely to have even more obvious consequences than in the past when they were often hidden behind growth phenomena. Likewise, reorganisations of the education system and variations in the demand for education can be considered as permanent features. It is not sufficient, therefore, simply to seek solutions, here and now, to the problems of surplus space. It is equally important to analyse the lessons to be learnt from past experience for future policies, and in this respect the present part of the report is of interest also to countries which have not yet experienced surplus.

Future educational facilities policies will have to assume two major tasks: first, minimize the development of future surplus so as to keep the unavoidable margin of surplus below crisis level; second, whatever the extent of emerging surplus, ensure the best possible use of the ressources it represents. Both tasks have implications for planning and design not only in terms of new building but also in relation to existing resources.

Planning Issues

In assuming these tasks, planners will be concerned less with adding to the stock and more with developing its capacity to respond rapidly and economically to fluctuations in needs.

Recent experiences provide an indication of the kind of planning approaches that might be adopted. For convenience sake, a distinction has been made between three main types of approaches. The first aims at dealing with peak enrolments as a temporary phenomenon not requiring investments in permanent facilities. The second concerns new ways of considering the interdependence between housing and facilities. The third consists in tackling the problems at the level of local facilities networks. Obviously, the three approaches are not mutually exclusive and can in fact be combined in different ways

according to context. Indeed, far more account will need to be taken in future planning of the diversity of local situations.

Dealing with *peak enrolments* consists in developing a system of temporary use of certain kinds of facilities and in promoting, in various ways, a more flexible use of the stock of facilities. The general recommendation in Australia to provide permanent accommodation for 80 per cent only of estimated maximum future enrolments constitutes a first move in this direction. A more elaborate example is the one developed in New Zealand where relocatable building units are used systematically to cope with local increases in enrolments, either in the form of entire schools or in a combination of such units with permanent buildings (there is, for example, a regulation stipulating that no primary school should accommodate more than 400 pupils in permanent buildings). In New Zealand the long tradition of relocating buildings, the high quality of its timber industry, and, above all, the existence of a highly developed transport and haulage trade with skilled personnel explain the wide application of this solution. A number of other countries have also used relocatable buildings and some have come up with technically and economically relatively satisfactory solutions. The New Zealand solution, however, attracts particular attention because of the scale on which it is used (more than 40 per cent of the stock of educational buildings is made up of such units and more than 5 per cent are actually moved each year) and because of the extent to which it forms an integral part of educational facilities planning[1].

Flexibility to cope rapidly and temporarily with peak enrolments needs not necessarily imply the use of demountable or relocatable buildings. In the United States, for instance, school districts with shortage of funds have a fairly long experience of limiting the capacity provided in permanent buildings to minimum enrolments by using other community facilities. This stems from the discovery that a large reservoir of public, semi-public and private spaces existed which could be used by the education system making superfluous some capital investments likely to prove unnecessary over time. Thus in Philadelphia, a flexible planning system has been in operation over the past ten years or so, in which a special real estate group is responsible, together with the Superintendent of Schools, for finding alternative accommodation in community and church-related facilities. Today, the education system has no difficulty in solving the problems arising from the considerable decline in enrolments: rented or borrowed accommodation returns to other uses and the full use of the facilities it owns is ensured. Temporary use of non-educational facilities may, of course, not always be a good or an inexpensive solution. What is important is the way in which this solution is integrated into facilities planning as a means of ensuring the flexibility of stock over a relatively long period.

A second type of approach concerns new ways of dealing with the *interdependence between housing and facilities.* School buildings have for a long time been built to meet needs arising from housing construction and their planning was thus entirely dependent on that of housing. The emergence of surplus shows that this relation of interdependence will need to change. The very rigid planning regulations which were developed in the past no longer fit the new situation. In France, for example, the Fifth Plan (1965-70) prescribed fixed modules for the size of schools in new residential areas; thus, according to the number of dwellings built, primary schools were to have a variable number of classes but always as a multiple of five (i.e. 5, 10, 15, 20 classes). The rigidity of this rule, since abandoned, and also the fact that it was applied generally over a fairly long period (even in areas for which it was never intented) largely explain the often rapid emergence of surplus space in this country. Today the need for more flexible planning approaches, better adapted to changing situations, is generally recognised.

One way of achieving such flexibility is to phase the construction of residential areas and/or provide different types of dwellings in such areas, a solution often advocated also for other reasons. One of the conclusions of the Västerås study was that the construction of new housing units should be timed in such a way that the increase in educational needs in the new neighbourhood coincided with a decrease in the older, adjacent areas; the need for new educational building could thus be significantly reduced.

Another solution consists in planning for future change of use. In some new settlements (e.g. Saint-Quentin-en-Yvelines, France and Upplands Väsby, Sweden), schools have been incorporated into housing units with the intention to turn them into flats when enrolments decrease. In the County of Essex, England, schools have been conceived for future conversion into other community facilities such as youth clubs or social centres. As will

be seen later, these solutions have important implications for the initial design of the facilities. On the south-west coast of France, in an area developed for tourism, an opposite approach has been adopted. Because of the proximity to Bordeaux the holiday residences now built will, in due course, become permanent residences, with a consequent need for schools. Therefore, some of the recreation facilities have been planned for later conversion into schools. In the transitional period (approximately ten years) they will serve, outside the tourist season, as field study or outdoor activity centres for schools in Bordeaux or other towns in the area.

The way in which the interdependence between housing and facilities is now conceived also increasingly affects urban renewal. Thus, the location, capacity and physical condition of existing facilities tend to become essential elements in any redevelopment plans and planners are faced with the task of integrating such facilities into their projects instead of purely and simply replacing them. The Inner London Education Authority, for instance, as part of a project to redevelop the Docklands, has evaluated the social infrastructure of the area. The aim was to give priority to the renovation and redevelopment of housing close to existing schools — many with spare capacity — so as to avoid unnecessary investments.

The last approach relates to the *transformation of facilities networks.* It essentially consists in creating, maintaining or re-establishing a balance in the provision of facilities between different zones in an area. It can take a number of forms: incentives to bussing, a new distribution of facilities for example between inner cities and suburbs, creation of a network of dispersed schools, development of support systems common to several schools or eventually establishing a new balance between facilities and communication systems.

The recommendation made by the State Board of Education in Michigan to increase transportation aid to districts using available accommodation in neighbouring districts instead of constructing new facilities provides an example of incentives to bussing. It should be noted, however, that such a measure in fact only constitutes a variation of the "transfer principle" and may have the same negative effects.

The interdependence of the decisions that need to be taken is particularly apparent in planning the distribution of facilities between inner cities and suburbs, especially in the case of upper secondary education as the following examples show.

In Milano, secondary schools in the city centre are old, obsolete and overcrowded, while at the same time their capacity exceeds the needs of the immediate neighbourhood, most of the pupils coming from the suburbs (Figure 23). This is also the case in Lisbon. The authorities therefore plan to decongest schools in the city centres by building a series of new schools in the suburbs. The purpose is to give peripheral districts greater autonomy and, by creating surplus capacity in the inner city schools, enable their working conditions to be improved. Whether a balance will develop over time depends on the behaviour of the school population. If the prestige of the inner city schools remains as high as at present, there is a risk that the schools in the periphery will be underutilised. In Stockholm, where there is surplus capacity in the inner city schools, the authorities resist the demand of peripheral districts wishing to have their own upper secondary schools. There is in fact every reason to believe that these would sooner or later in turn become surplus.

The concentration of facilities into large central schools, a favourite solution in the 1960s, is no longer accepted by the public. There is therefore a trend towards the organisation of networks within which a group of small, dispersed schools can offer all the various options and educational choices needed. School authorities in the United States, e.g. in Chicago and New York (Roosevelt Island) are rediscovering the virtues of small schools and decentralised school systems and have attempted to combine specialised "magnet schools" with general "satellite schools", which often also contain neighbourhood facilities (Figure 24). A similar pattern has been followed in Rødøy, Norway (Figure 25) near the Polar Circle, an area with low density, scattered population where educational provision for the last two years of compulsory education (grades 8 and 9) in a central school has recently been abolished. Recognizing that transportation over rough waters is often an ordeal, that boarding seems to affect personality growth negatively and that local communities were impoverished as a result of losing their teen-agers, those in charge of the project have preferred to introduce a decentralised system: in each locality the school has been reopened, and is organised on the basis of multi-age groups and a curriculum adapted to the life of the community[2].

A complementary approach consists in developing a system of support common to a number of schools, instead of providing each school with all the facilities it needs. When the network is concentrated, for instance in the case of a city, a common facility could be provided located at an approximately equal distance of the schools composing the network, e.g. a drama and arts workshop such as the Cockpit Theatre in London, a common library and resource centre or a specialised, vocational training centre such as the Skills Centers in the United States. When the network is dispersed over a thinly populated area, provision would rather take the form of mobile units bringing to the isolated schools within it specialised equipment, audio-visual material, documentation and the services of specially qualified teachers. This alternative has been used successfully in Auvergne, France, and in Germany. The value of such support systems resides in the possibility they offer to provide schools with services which each taken individually could not otherwise afford: they also contribute to developing communications between the schools and are obviously less vulnerable to fluctuating enrolments.

One of the main planning tasks in the future will no doubt consist in determining the balance to be achieved between facilities on the one hand and support and communication systems on the other. Certain promising experiences, e.g. in the field of adult education, such as the "Open University" in

Figure 23. **Present and Projected Capacity for Upper Secondary Education in the 20 School Districts of Milano**

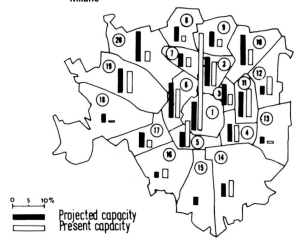

0   5   10%

■ Projected capacity
☐ Present capacity

Source: G. Leonardi, "Locazione e Fabbisogno", *Casabella No. 471*, September 1975.

Figure 24. Units of the Dispersed School on Roosevelt Island, Integrated into the Central Shopping Area and Multistorey Housing, New York

Satellite school

Swimming pool

Magnet school

Figure 25. **Reintroducing a Decentralised Pattern of Educational Provision at Compulsory School Level in Rødøy, Norway**

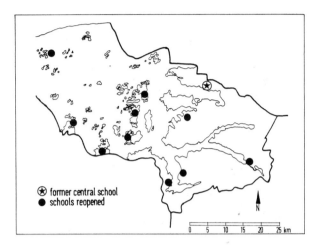

★ former central school
● schools reopened

0 5 10 15 20 25 km

N

Source: Olav Kvikne Tronvoll, "Rødøy-prosjektet – a Summary of Information on the Development of the Rødy Project", Report No. 5, Oslo, June 1977.

the United Kingdom, the "Edutrain" which allows workers from New York suburbs to use the time they spend on transport for educational activities, or "Learning Exchange" experiences such as the one developed in Evanston, Illinois (Figure 26), even leads to questioning whether the current balance between facilities and communication systems will not be radically reversed in the future.

Design Issues

Even if it is particularly difficult to dissociate planning and design in the efforts made to reuse existing surplus space or to prevent the emergence of surplus in the future, design has a specific role to play which needs to be spelt out. How can design help solve the problem of surplus school accommodation and, conversely, how does the need to prevent future surplus modify design?

Reusing surplus space or adjusting facilities to changing needs will necessitate transformation, adaptation or conversion. Some transformations, for example those which do not affect the structure or fabric of the building, can be made by the users themselves. This is, in fact, what happens in several countries and there are many examples of such transformations. Should such self-help remain a marginal practice or should it become a

key idea in facilities policies? Its positive effects on the participation of users in the life of an establishment and on user appropriation of space for work and leisure should not be underestimated. It is also of interest insofar as it allows a finer adjustment of facilities to needs. But self-help implies that pupils, teachers, parents or new user groups through voluntary participation take on responsibilities not only for execution but also for design. Therefore, the question arises as to the limits of their skills, although, here again, it would not be wise to make too hasty a judgement. Some projects have achieved real quality. This is the case in particular in vocational training institutions or whenever the tasks of transformation have an element of continuity and can allow self-help to be combined with an input of professionals. In the case of Marion High School, Australia, the progressive reuse of surplus space as soon as it emerges, has implied a continuous transformation of the facilities, associating self-help and the work of professionals, and there is no doubt whatever that the results are most satisfactory.

If this empirical approach is to be given a status because of its undeniable value, it will need to be given support. The fact that transformations undertaken on the basis of self-help cost less should not lead to considering them as cheap solutions. Financial aid is thus necessary but the support should also consist in stimulating initiatives, organising exchanges between them, and providing design and technical guidance. This is what certain Australian authorities are doing and groups of architects and technicians are specialising in this area, thus preparing for the self-help movement to become an integral part of their educational building policies (Figure 27). A prerequisite to the development of self-help is the organisation of some sort of control to provide reasonable guarantees in respect of quality and security. This support role which will generally be assumed by professionals — especially architects — is different from that which they have traditionally played.

Professionals will also be directly and more extensively involved in more important conversions necessitating, for example, a modification of the building structure or a complete remodelling of existing facilities. Here again, technical problems or design issues are often less critical than the change in attitudes and procedures which this type of work requires. Many architects because of their past experience tend to prefer new building

Figure 26.   Teacher, Learner and Interest Cards from the Learning Exchange, Evanston, Illinois

<u>NEW REGISTRANT POST CARD</u>

> Dear New Registrant,
>
>   Welcome to The Learning Exchange! Your registration form has been received and processed. You are now entitled to use The Learning Exchange anytime during our 68-hour week (Mon.-Fri. 9 am-9 pm; Sat. 9 am-5 pm). Just give us a call at 273-3383 to let us know what you want to learn, teach, or share.
>   Thanks again for registering with The Learning Exchange. We look forward to serving you soon!
>
>   Sincerely yours,
>
>   *Edward R. Dobmeyer*
>   Edward R. Dobmeyer
>   Manager of Operations

<u>COMPLETED LEARNER CARD</u>

Topic SPANISH	1 Zone

Description, Competency, & Level
Going to Brazil in November — wants to learn Spanish from a native speaker.

Name, City, & Zip Code	Phones & Best Time To Call
John Doe	360-3312 (evenings)
Evanston 60202	290-4420 (days)

Date 6/10/77	Fee: Ⓨ N M no more than $5/hr.	Willing To Travel Yes - no more than 15 miles	Staff B.J.

<u>COMPLETED TEACHER CARD</u>

Topic Welding	1 Zone

Description, Competency, & Level Has been a welder
for 16 years — willing to teach beginning through advanced — prefers to teach on a one-to-one basis.

Name, City, & Zip Code	Phones & Best Time To Call
John Doe	360-3312 (evenings)
Evanston, 60202	290-4420 (days)

Date 6/10/77	Fee: Ⓨ N M $5.00/hr.	Willing To Travel Yes - no more than 10 miles	Staff B.J.

<u>COMPLETED INTEREST MATCH CARD</u>

Topic TENNIS	1 Zone

Description, Competency, & Level
Looking for players on the intermediate level.

Name, City, & Zip Code	Phones & Best Time To Call
John Doe	360-3312 (evenings)
Evanston 60202	290-4420 (days)

Date 6/10/77	Fee Ⓨ N M For court time	Willing To Travel Yes - 5 miles	Staff B.J.

<u>PARTIALLY COMPLETED FEEDBACK CARD "A"</u>

NAME John Doe		✔ CHECK MEMBER	CALL BACK DATE 6/24/77
PHONE/BEST TIME TO CALL 360-3312 (evenings) 290-4420 (days)	CITY Evanston	ZONE 1	
WE CALLED ☐ THEY CALLED ☐ BOTH ☐ RETURNED OUR CALL ☐ DATES DONE			

TOPIC / NAME	TLI	SUB	COMMENTS
Welding / J. Peterson	L		
Welding / F. Zillo	L		
Spanish / R. Jones	T		
Spanish / B. Thompson	T		
Tennis / J. Adams	I		

NOTE ANY ACTION TAKEN FOR EACH SUBJECT LISTED AND ADDITIONAL COMMENTS ON REVERSE SIDE OF CARD	Staff B.J.

Source: G. Robert Lewis and Diane Reiko Kinishi, "The Learning Exchange: What it is, how it works and how you can set up a similar program for your community", Evanston, Illinois, 1977.

Figure 27.   Introduction to the Self-help Manual produced by the Government Architects Branch, New South Wales, Australia

PRODUCED BY SCHOOLS SECTION
GOVERNMENT ARCHITECTS BRANCH, P.W.D., N.S.W.
FUNDED BY SCHOOLS COMMISSION

THIS EDITION OF THE SELF HELP MANUAL HAS BEEN PRINTED WITH THE AID OF A
SCHOOLS COMMISSION GRANT, ON THE ADVICE OF THE BUILDINGS COMMITTEE, AS A MEANS
OF ENABLING SCHOOLS THROUGHOUT AUSTRALIA TO COME INTO CONTACT WITH IDEAS WHICH
COULD CONTRIBUTE TO AN IMPROVEMENT IN THEIR PHYSICAL ENVIRONMENTS.

INTRODUCTION

THIS 'MANUAL' IS A COLLECTION OF IDEAS FOR AND ABOUT SCHOOLS.   MOST OF
THE IDEAS RELATE TO THE USE OF SPACE, THE BUILDINGS AND THE GROUNDS, AND
UNDERLYING THEM ALL IS A DESIRE TO EXTEND AND IMPROVE THE WAY WE USE OUR SCHOOLS.

WHEREVER POSSIBLE WE HAVE CHOSEN IDEAS WHICH HAVE ALREADY BEEN TRIED AND
ARE CAPABLE OF IMPLEMENTATION CHEAPLY WITHOUT EXPENSIVE EQUIPMENT OR HIGHLY
SKILLED LABOUR.   HENCE THE TITLE "SELF HELP".   NOT ONLY IS IT ESSENTIAL THAT
THE IDEAS BE EASILY IMPLEMENTED, BUT IT IS IMPORTANT THAT EACH PROJECT IS SEEN
AS A LEARNING EXPERIENCE IN ITSELF.   THE PROCESS OF PRODUCING SOMETHING FOR YOUR
OWN SCHOOL HELPS BREAKDOWN THE FEELING OF ALIENATION AND LACK OF IDENTIFICATION
WHICH MARKS MANY OF OUT INSTITUTIONS.

THE SCHOOLS SECTION OF THE GOVERNMENT ARCHITECTS BRANCH IS RESPONSIBLE FOR
THE DESIGN OF SCHOOLS IN N.S.W. AND SUBSEQUENTLY IT IS OF PARTICULAR CONCERN TO
SEE THE WAYS IN WHICH PEOPLE USE THE BUILDINGS PRODUCED.   WITH THE ADVENT OF
MORE COMPLEX BUILDINGS WE HAVE ACCEPTED THE RESPONSIBILITY FOR INFORMING THE
USERS ABOUT WAYS IN WHICH THE BUILDINGS MAY BE BETTER USED.   SIMILARLY, THERE IS
A RESPONSIBILITY TO BRING OUR SKILLS TO THE GREATER PROPORTION OF EXISTING SCHOOLS
WHICH COULD BENEFIT FROM SMALL SCALE INNOVATION.

WE HAVEN'T TRIED TO BE EXHAUSTIVE, OR DEFINITIVE, IN OUR COLLECTION OF IDEAS,
RATHER IT IS A MIXTURE OF FAR-FETCHED DREAMS WITH MUNDANE, SIMPLE PROJECTS, ALL
THROWN TOGETHER IN A CASUAL WAY (MOST OF THE FAR-FETCHED DREAMS HAVE BEEN BUILT).

THIS MANUAL IS DESIGNED TO BE RIPPED UP AND PASSED AROUND THE STAFF ROOM,
INDIVIDUAL SHEETS USED AS POSTERS, CUT OUT AND ADDED TO.   (WRITE TO US FOR MORE
COPIES).   IT IS NOT A FINISHED DOCUMENT.   WE ARE KEEN TO SEE WHETHER TEACHERS
NEED THIS KIND OF SERVICE AND WE WANT CONTRIBUTIONS TO THE MANUAL.   JUST WRITE-UP
A FLOOSCAP SHEET ON YOUR IDEA AND SEND IT TO US.   IF YOU NEED PERSONAL CONTACT
WITH AN ARCHITECT OR LANDSCAPER OR INTERIOR DESIGNER OR ENGINEER PLEASE CONTACT US.

Source: The Self Help Manual, produced by the Schools Section, Government Architects Branch, Public Works Department, Sydney, August 1978.

projects to the difficult modesty implied in conversion and renovation, all the more so as usually neither prestige nor income are proportionate to the hardly visible work on details such projects demand.

There are nevertheless examples which give valuable indications of the importance and specificity of the role of the designers in conversion. In Grand Rapids, Michigan, plans for the remodelling of a central school site which accommodated three schools, originally provided for sports fields (football, baseball, athletics) and more parking spaces. When the high school was declared surplus the architect engaged for the remodelling initiated a participatory design process which involved all interested groups in the community wanting to advise the education authorities. As a result of this process, the site was transformed into a landscaped community park with a playground for elementary school children, a nature area, a gymnasium and swimming pool for joint school and community use, and the former high school became a community centre. To quote one of the planners in the school administration, the outcome could not be predicted: "Had I gone through the standard planning process we would have on the site what I initially indicated, and not seen these new possibilities"[3]. It is the work and participatory planning process of the designer which in such a case become the key to the decisions that are taken. It is this approach which revealed the potential of the existing resources to satisfy local needs which it also helped to identify.

A final remark needs to be made in relation to conversion of facilities: there are numerous examples of buildings whose occupancy changes a number of times and which thus enjoy several new lives once they have ceased to serve their original purposes. Consequently, the transformation of facilities to meet new needs can be regarded as a continuous process which should not be stopped by solutions that are so definite that they freeze all possibilities of subsequent conversion.

When it is no longer a matter of adapting buildings to new needs but to design new buildings to be added to the stock, another type of design issue arises. The question of how to provide for future change has been in the minds of designers long before the problems of surplus space arose. The study, undertaken a few years ago by PEB on this question made a clear distinction between adaptability and flexibility[4]. While its recommendation for providing flexibility through variety of space rather than providing costly structural adaptability has proved to be correct, the type of change discussed related only to variations in group size and to a widening of the range of educational activities. It has subsequently become clear that fluctuating enrolments and rapid changes in student options create additional design problems, especially in the area of vocational training. Further research will be needed therefore to make the findings of this study applicable also to far more varied situations.

Accommodating other than educational activities and users in schools implies joint and shared use of spaces and raises yet another type of problem for design, more closely related to those discussed in the series of PEB studies on facilities co-ordination[5]. The large educational and community centres built in many countries in the 1960s and early 1970s represented a first attempt to overcome these problems. By providing a variety of spaces for different user groups and facilitating communication between activities, these projects aimed at satisfying a multiplicity of needs in a single set of facilities. The possibility these solutions offered in terms of adjusting to future variations in needs only came as an afterthought. However, the size of the projects and their institutional nature have often prevented the identity and character of different user groups to be expressed. The need to define territories more clearly and to give expression to specific traits through design will thus become increasingly important in the future.

Since, a new type of solution has emerged which is more specifically directed towards preventing future surplus. It is a question of predicting for new buildings — schools for example — the future uses to which they will be put, uses that are different from those for which they are designed at the outset. Reference to this type of solution was made already in relation to planning. Some further examples will underline its design aspects. In a number of cases schools have been designed for later conversion into housing or community facilities (Figures 28-29). Besides the ease of conversion these solutions represent, they have the advantage of procuring a domestic character to the school which is important for young children. They also favour closer relations between the school and the neighbourhood encouraging community use of school workshops and recreation facilities.

Figure 28. Integration of Housing and Primary School in Grimstaby, Upplands Väsby, Sweden

PLAN OF NEIGHBOURHOOD BLOCK 1

Source: Upplands Väsby Kommun, "Integrerade serviceanläggningar i Upplands Väsby", brochure prepared for OECD/PEB Symposium on
Co-ordination of School and Community Facilities, Sweden, September 1976.

Entrance to classrooms which are situated on the ground floor, the flats above have their own entrance from the road

Figure 29. School Designed in Separate Blocks to Allow Gradual Conversion into Community Facilities and/or Housing, Lowton High School, Wigan, Lancashire

In these particular examples, where the initial use for school purposes is considered as a stage in a development towards a future, previously defined use, designers are faced with the problem of reconciling the design characteristics of the initial use with those of the intended future use. They also have to decide to what extent the future use, which is by no means certain, should form part of the initial design brief. The recommendation made in the PEB study on adaptability and flexibility that provision for future change should not be at the expense of sacrificing present needs remains valid also in relation to these new issues.

In countries where the use of relocatable units seems to be a viable or necessary solution in planning terms, a serious effort will need to be made to develop designs which reconcile technical and economic considerations with qualitative improvements to satisfy educational needs better and achieve a better integration into the environment. Even where technically satisfactory results have been obtained — for example, in Germany with a component system whose grid-structure allows a great variety of plan forms or in New Zealand with the development of combinable units — relocatable buildings still remain a relatively unsatisfactory solution from the standpoint of design. In the New Zealand experience, the frequent combination of relocatable and permanent buildings had led to a somewhat paradoxical situation: to match building styles, it is the type and form of the permanent buildings which have been adjusted to those of the relocatable buildings and not the other way round.

Design issues can never be dissociated from cost considerations. In the case of conversion or renovation for which strict expenditure norms can hardly be established, designers rarely work within precise cost limits. Instead, it is often incumbent on them to propose solutions which because of their cost are credible and may be preferred to the more radical — and often more attractive — solution of building anew. The relationship between cost and design, however, becomes far more complex when in the case of a new building one foresees many different uses for it in the course of its life span. It is likely that in the future the cost of a building will need to be calculated not over the short-term by limiting the assessment to initial capital costs, but over its total life cycle.

NOTES

1. "Relocatable Schools in New Zealand", *Information Leaflet No. 12,* OECD/PEB, Paris, 1982.

2. Olav Kvikne Tronvoll, "Rødøyprosjektet — A Summary of Information on the Development of the Rødøy Project", Report No. 5, Oslo, June 1977.

3. Aase Eriksen and Caroline Spankie, "Final Report to Central Park Committee", Grand Rapids, Michigan, 1978.

4. *Adaptability.* The quality of a building which facilitates adaptation; adaptation may require relocation, replacement, removal or addition in respect of either the constructional elements, services or the finishes of the building — essentially large magnitude/low frequency change.
    Flexibility. The quality of a building which permits variation in the activities, timetabling, class size, etc., of a school without the need for adaptation as defined — essentially low magnitude/high frequency change.
    Providing for Future Change — Adaptatibility and Flexibility in School Building, OECD/PEB, Paris, 1976.

5. *Building for School and Community, Vol. I-V, op. cit.*

Part six

SUMMARY OF CONCLUSIONS

Under the combined effects of diminishing pressures to meet basic needs for new pupil places and severe economic constraints future educational policies will to a large extent be governed by the need to redeploy resources. Compared to other resources, however, buildings are specific insofar as they are fixed assets. Decisions concerning their redeployment need to be based on different considerations than those governing, for example, the redeployment of teachers. This does not mean, however, that the two are not interdependent.

The current stock of educational buildings represents a great potential. To exploit this fully, it is not enough simply to consider how the stock can be made to match current needs, quantitatively as well as qualitatively. It demands an anticipation of how these needs will evolve and an exploration also of what other needs existing facilities can help meet. It thus raises the question as to whether the redeployment of available educational building resources should be limited to the education sector only, by "internal" redeployment between different types and levels of education, or be extended to cover needs of other social sectors as well.

Any policy for the redeployment of physical resources is thus dependent for its implementation on a number of conditions. The way in which these are fulfilled and the priorities to be set will vary from country to country. By and large, however, and the present report provides ample evidence of this, the problems to be faced and the practical considerations to be taken into account seem to be similar everywhere. These have therefore been summarized below in the form of a number of strategy pointers.

School Population Change

The impact of economic, technological, social and demographic change on education and on the level and nature of demand for educational facilities is likely to become even greater and more difficult to forecast than in the recent past. Effective resource planning will thus depend on the extent to which a better understanding can be gained of the reasons for changes in the school population.

Local situations vary considerably as the existence side by side of surplus space and over-crowding in schools clearly illustrates. It is evident therefore that *population statistics and forecasts,* if they are to become effective planning tools in situations characterized by rapid change, need to be more refined and localised (cf. efforts made in this direction in for example, Grampian Region, Scotland; Ontario, Canada; Västerås, Sweden). Such forecasts will also need to be supplemented by *analyses of other factors affecting demographic change, such as likely economic and social trends.* Here again, data will have to be localised but set in their broader regional, national and sometimes international context.

The extent to which the collection and interpretation of data can be carried out locally depends on the skills and resources at the disposal of local authorities. In cases where these tasks have to be assumed, in whole or in part, by regional and/or central authorities or where local data are fed into a centralised system, it is essential to ensure that local authorities have easy and rapid access to the relevant data (cf. the information system developed in Ontario). Besides a more systematic dissemination of information to local authorities there is a need to develop the methods and skills needed to undertake local assessments.

Capacity and Potential of Building Stock

Population data and analyses of the reasons for fluctuations in school enrolments are meaningful only insofar as they are related to existing capacity. They need therefore to be accompanied by an *evaluation of the educational building stock.* The purpose of such evaluation is to estimate the value of the stock for meeting current and, even more important, future needs. This value cannot be expressed in financial terms alone. To be useful, it will need to be assessed in terms of a number of indicators of quantity and types of accommodation, suitability for the purposes served, physical condition and remodelling potential, energy demand and other aspects of running costs, and finally value to the community.

There are two levels at which stock evaluation is needed: first, at the local or regional level which in most situations is the level at which decisions are taken on the reorganisation of school networks or the remodelling of facilities to accommodate new needs; second, at the national or state level to serve as a basis for overall policy decisions or decisions on appropriate levels of financing. (*A Study of School Building* is an excellent example of such a national evaluation). In both cases stock evaluation is a forecasting tool but the kind of information sought and the way in which it is collected will vary according to the objective pursued. The closer to the local level, the more detailed and practical the evaluation needs to be.

What is important is that a first start is made, even with crude and simple methods. With time and experience these can be refined and the range of facilities covered by the evaluation extended to include also other than educational facilities. As demographic change occurs, there will be a growing need to consider all public buildings in a community as a single stock. Reorganisation of such an overall network of community facilities is not only dependent on a wider evaluation of stock, it represents in fact the point at which stock evaluation becomes integral with stock management and interactive with the forecasting of needs.

Actual, Potential and Future Needs of the Community

While it seems natural to consider *educational needs* first, it should be borne in mind that these may not necessarily always be the most pressing. The education sector was for a long time one of the most privileged public sectors and during that period a number of other social needs were not met. Surplus space in schools provides an opportunity to make up for part of this backlog.

To *remedy deficiencies and improve working conditions* in schools which do not meet current standards is a natural first option. But using surplus space for improvements that go far beyond the average standards of the stock as a whole may not only prove prohibitive in terms of unit costs but may also lead to claims for the "new" standards to be extended to the stock as a whole and to become the general norm. Education authorities must therefore carefully consider the consequences of such improvements, in particular the degree of autonomy to be granted to individual schools to use available space as they see fit.

There may in fact be other needs that are more urgent. These may concern the diversification of educational provision, i.e. meeting the growing demand for nursery education, new types of education and training at the post-compulsory level, adult education, education for the handicapped, etc., or they may relate to the creation of services common to a network of education institutions, e.g. field study centres, resource centres, computer centres, skill centres, drama and arts centres, teacher centres, etc.

Consequently, any assessment of educational needs implies *policy choices and co-operation* between various sectors of the education system, between neighbouring school districts or regions and between all those concerned including the users. It requires a clear understanding of the overall costs involved.

Faced with falling enrolments and rising unit costs authorities are sometimes tempted to apply in a fairly mechanical way what is known as the "transfer principle" i.e. transferring pupils in such a way that in the case of two half-empty schools in an area, one becomes full and the other empty. Although the "transfer principle" aims at ensuring that no school's enrolment falls below a threshold considered educationally or economically viable, a policy based on this principle is open to serious objections. First is the risk of depriving the community of an important element in local life and of increasing the difficulties (and costs) involved in transporting pupils. Secondly, concentrating the school network often results in large schools and in a need for extensions. Finally, if the empty school has to be "mothballed" to keep it in reserve for any future upturn in enrolments, the economic advantage of closure is partly offset by the fact that the buildings have to be maintained and heated to some degree; empty buildings are also more prone to vandalism.

Thus, instead of concentrating the school network, it may in many cases be more advantageous to aim at consolidating it. This would imply that the individual buildings making up the network would serve for school use as well as for other purposes. The reduced number of pupils would occupy part of the premises only whereas redundant accommodation and/or land would be lent, let or sold as appropriate to meet other needs — educational, social, cultural or economic. This approach may make a certain number of school closures unnecessary, contribute to providing funds for improvements or for reducing recurrent costs and, in the case of leasing, serve as an insurance against any future upturn in enrolments. Such joint use of premises can also be of considerable benefit to education itself.

It is important therefore to consider also *other than educational needs* and to enable public agencies, voluntary groups, associations, trades, small industry as well as non-organised groups in the community requiring accommodation for their activities to express their needs. It may sometimes even be necessary to employ people to work with the community to ensure that needs and opportunities are fully appreciated. Many examples are given in the present report showing the range of possible uses for surplus school accommodation (cf. the typology of uses outlined in Part Three) and various approaches to assessing non-educational needs (e.g. the Parallel Use Committees in Toronto and the special facilities co-ordinator in Montgomery County, Maryland).

Participation in Decision-making and Incentives

Having analysed the likely nature of future change, determined the capacity and characteristics of the existing stock and assessed the need for accommodation for educational and other purposes, a choice has to be made among a series of possible options. Such a choice may relate to an individual school but experience suggests that the most appropriate level for dealing with these problems is that of a network of schools in a district or region. Any decisions on redeployment require for their success, a commitment from those directly concerned. To achieve this it is necessary to develop a process which allows more people to take part in decisions and provides for wide consultation within the community, e.g. in the form of public hearings, enquiries, etc.

Such a process hinges on better and more widely disseminated information, in particular as regards the cost implications and relative advantages and disadvantages of various options.

There are numerous examples to show that technocratic blue-prints imposed on a population by an authority result in protests and distrust, particularly when they involve the closing down of schools. Redeployment measures must tend towards better solutions overall and their acceptance will often depend on the incentives provided. These can be in the form of improved working conditions, a better quality of education or of the built environment, a closer relation between the school and the community, or an opportunity to meet hitherto neglected needs. None of these things can however be achieved without some financial incentives which may range from limited aid to self-help to the possibility for a local authority to use the proceeds from leasing or sale to improve the quality of provision.

Financial Procedures, Norms and Regulations

Current systems of *financing,* which in the majority of countries are still tied to the provision of new pupil places, constitute serious obstacles to the development of effective policies for the transformation of the existing stock. New procedures will be needed which permit the financing of adaptations and renovations, facilitate co-ordination, contribute to reducing recurrent costs and provide the necessary incentives for the most effective management of resources.

Such a shift of emphasis within capital budgets will need to be accompanied by a reconsideration of the way in which the financial burden is shared between various levels of authority. Situations in which local authorities often have to assume a larger share of the costs for transformation than for new building and where sectoral accountability for funds impedes appropriate solutions for sharing space must be reviewed. Whatever form the new measures take (state subsidies, block grants, increased capacity for self-finance at local level, etc.) particular attention needs to be paid to the problem of the fair distribution of resources so that poor municipalities are not put at disadvantage.

Like financing procedures, current *norms and standards* are in most countries geared towards new building. Consequently, they cannot easily be applied to the very diverse situations of reuse or conversion. There is therefore a need to be flexible and allow a much wider margin of interpretation. Use of resources cannot, however, be governed solely by the characteristics of individual situations. Therefore, new types of norms and standards applicable to renovation and adaptation will need to be developed. They will probably have to be formulated in terms of minimum and maximum requirements and a hierarchy of priorities to be followed when it comes to improving working conditions or adapting facilities to new needs. Likewise, norms and standards for new buildings will need to be revised at regular intervals to allow solutions to be developed which more than in the past facilitate future change.

The most difficult problem to solve is likely to be the development of *control systems* which take into account both the flexibility needed to respond to very diverse situations and the necessity to ensure that available resources are used equitably and effectively. Such systems will probably involve *a posteriori* rather than *a priori* control and have to be based more than in the past on the monitoring of experiences and evaluation of their potential.

Finally, *laws and regulations* have often not been adapted to suit the new situations and often impede appropriate solutions from being developed. The focus in the past has been on simplifying the procedures for closing and selling schools, an essentially negative option. What is needed in the future are positive measures to overcome problems of ownership, facilitate joint use, define legal responsibilities more clearly and make adequate insurance arrangements.

Roles and Attitudes

Because of the diversity of situations and the need to deal with these primarily at local level, the traditional roles exercised by central, regional and local authorities in educational building will need to be considerably modified. The experiences described in the present report show that to be effective decisions on reuse, renovation, extension and new provision will increasingly have to be taken at the local level. Therefore, whenever this is not yet the case, the decision-making power in facilities policies will need to be transferred to *local authorities* (or if these are too small, to a consortium of local authorities or a regional authority). This presupposes that they are given the legal, administrative and financial means necessary to act and that new types of relations, based on co-operation rather than control, are developed with the authorities next in the hierarchy (whether regional or central). It also means that appropriate co-ordination mechanisms have to be developed at local level allowing horizontal links to be established between services and institutions and enabling the users and the public concerned to make their voice heard.

Under these circumstances the main role of the *central authorities* which politically remain responsible for the equitable distribution of funds and for ensuring that the quality of the public service is maintained will be to:

— Collate, analyse and disseminate information on new uses of existing facilities, on the potential which redeployment and transformation of stock represents and on ways and means of preventing future surplus or providing for future change;

— Put at the disposal of local authorities the specific skills that they may need (e.g. in the field of evaluation) and help develop such skills at local level;

— Apply a continuous incentives policy to develop and support local initiatives; such incentives should not only be financial (aid to self-help, new modes of allocating resources, decompartmentalisation of financial procedures, block grants, etc.) but also legal and administrative (to facilitate transfer of ownership, promote participation in decision-making, develop new norms and guidelines, etc.);

— Undertake a continuous effort of research and development, focusing essentially on the reorganisation of networks, the reuse and conversion of existing facilities and the maximisation of the potential they represent but including work also on such planning and design issues relative to new building which could contribute to minimising future surplus.

A change of roles is in itself insufficient and needs to be accompanied by a *change of attitudes* on the part of all concerned. Solutions to the problems will depend on the ability of people to exercise their responsibilities with foresight and imagination and unconstrained by past habits and policies, devised for situations that no longer exist. If redeployment policies are to succeed, they will need to be developed as joint ventures in which surplus space is seen as a major opportunity for bringing about a substantial improvement to the stock of buildings for education and other social purposes and to create new relationships between school and community.

CASE STUDIES

Identity: Ontario one of the largest and wealthiest provinces of Canada with 8.26 million inhabitants. Its industrial and administrative center Toronto grew from 600 000 to 2 500 000 inhabitants within a few decades.

Main reasons for surplus space: Lowering of fertility rate, birth decline and halted immigration from outside Canada as well as interprovincial population flows.

Quantity of surplus space in 1977: 382 110 places in elementary, 100 375 in secondary, 150 605 in separate Roman Catholic schools; a total of 633 090 places. Between 1970 and 1977 a total of 900 schools have been closed (excluding private schools).

Uses of surplus school spaces: Recreation, social services, conversion to private residences or housing for senior citizens.

Authorities concerned: Mainly local school boards, unions and the State Ministry of Education.

Most important points: State-wide process for investigating the scope and effects of declining enrolments, initiated through a royal one man commission; involvement of all participants in the discussion; comprehensive publication of all issues considered important in 84 reports and papers.

Context

The Province of Ontario provides one of the few state-wide examples of a comprehensive approach to dealing with the effects of declining enrolments. The 1960s represented a decade of educational expansion during which Canada ranked first among the highly industrialised nations as a spender on public education (as a per cent of GNP)[1] and Ontario first among the Canadian Provinces[2].

From the mid-1970s declining enrolments began to be seen as a policy problem but also as an opportunity to cut back a public sector which for long had received a disproportionate share of public resources. One of the traditional means of Government to focus public attention and open a public debate on an important policy issue is to appoint a Royal Commission. Such a One Man Commission on Declining Enrolments (CODE) was established in August 1977.

One of the first moves of the Commissioner, Dr. R.W.B. Jackson, was to contact all powerful educational groups in the Province to solicit their co-operation. The most important among these were: the Ontario Teachers' Federation, the Ontario School Trustees Council, the Ontario Association of Educational Administration Officials and the Federation of Home and School Clubs (PTAs). Further moves included the formation of various task forces and the organisation of public hearings everywhere in the Province. By the end of 1978, CODE had produced a total of 84 publications.

Although CODE was not the first to deal with the problem of declining enrolments, the establishment of the Commission received far more public attention than any previous moves and also gave rise to what in retrospect can be said to have been excessive expectations that something could be done immediately to attenuate the effects of decline.

The first task was to choose among various population projections (Figure 1) that which seemed to be the most likely and which could serve as a basis for decisions at the state level. Within the two years of CODE's investigation the situation turned out to be worse than expected. The average family size of 1.5 children was the lowest anticipated; in addition, interprovincial migration for Ontario turned negative during

Figure 1. **Projected School Enrolment Age Groups to Year 2001**

In Thousands

Year	Projection 1		Projection 2		Projection 3		Projection 4	
	5-13	14-18	5-13	14-18	5-13	14-18	5-13	14-18
Actual 1976 Census	1 302.4	815.9	1 302.4	815.9	1 302.4	815.9	1 302.4	815.9
1977	1 272.1	827.9	1 270.0	827.0	1 270.0	827.0	1 267.8	826.0
1978	1 241.5	834.6	1 236.4	832.3	1 237.1	832.7	1 232.5	830.6
1979	1 214.3	832.2	1 205.1	827.9	1 206.8	828.9	1 199.5	825.7
1980	1 200.0	814.6	1 185.9	807.8	1 189.5	809.8	1 179.0	805.1
1981	1 192.8	795.1	1 172.9	785.5	1 178.7	788.6	1 164.8	782.4
1982	1 203.4	765.5	1 176.7	752.9	1 182.5	757.4	1 164.6	749.3
1983	1 218.5	737.9	1 184.4	722.1	1 188.2	727.9	1 166.3	718.0
1984	1 232.0	720.9	1 189.6	701.8	1 189.9	709.3	1 163.8	697.5
1985	1 246.6	715.1	1 195.9	692.5	1 190.9	701.5	1 160.7	687.9
1986	1 272.7	709.5	1 212.8	683.2	1 201.1	693.9	1 166.6	678.4
1987	1 305.2	708.8	1 234.7	678.6	1 216.1	691.3	1 177.3	673.7
1988	1 343.3	706.1	1 262.5	672.1	1 235.3	686.6	1 192.0	667.0
1989	1 381.1	701.2	1 289.3	663.3	1 252.4	679.8	1 204.6	658.0
1990	1 423.8	692.9	1 320.3	650.9	1 271.8	669.4	1 219.5	645.8
1991	1 459.3	701.6	1 344.2	655.0	1 285.3	672.7	1 228.7	647.0
1992	1 492.6	717.1	1 365.8	665.7	1 297.0	680.7	1 236.1	652.8
1993	1 522.9	739.0	1 385.0	682.6	1 305.8	692.7	1 241.1	662.7
1994	1 549.8	761.2	1 401.1	699.1	1 312.0	702.8	1 243.6	670.5
1995	1 573.3	788.4	1 414.7	720.1	1 315.8	716.0	1 243.7	681.2
1996	1 593.1	809.7	1 424.3	734.9	1 315.8	724.8	1 240.8	687.2
1997	1 608.1	830.5	1 430.4	748.8	1 312.9	733.6	1 234.9	698.7
1998	1 617.7	850.7	1 431.8	762.3	1 306.9	742.1	1 226.3	699.9
1999	1 622.0	870.0	1 428.6	775.1	1 298.4	750.1	1 215.5	705.5
2000	1 622.3	887.9	1 422.2	786.8	1 288.0	756.6	1 202.6	710.0
2001	1 618.9	903.9	1 412.9	796.8	1 276.6	761.2	1 189.4	712.4

Source : The Commission on Declining Enrolments in Ontario, *Implication of Declining Enrolment for the Schools of Ontario : A Statement of Effects and Solutions,* Final Report, Toronto, october 1978.

1978. In October 1978, the Commission in its final report pointed out that it seemed quite possible that elementary school enrolments would continue to decline until 1990 and secondary school enrolments well beyond the year 2000 (Figure 2).

It was recognized, however, that this overall picture was by no means typical of every local situation. Generally speaking, each school board found that its own problems were unique and that it had to develop its own solutions to respond to local needs. While some boards experienced stable or even increasing enrolments, others faced quite a different situation resulting from population shifts owing to growing land prices or a receding industry.

The major problems created by declining enrolments were associated by the Commission with programmes, staffing and facilities. In this case

study, the focus will be on the facilities aspects.

Figure 2. **The Most Likely Population, Elementary and Secondary School Enrolment Trends, Ontario, 1981 to 2001**

In Millions

Year	Population			Projected enrolment	
	Age groups		All age groups (zero to 85+)	Element-ary	Second-ary
	5 to 14	15 to 19			
1976	1.47	0.81	8.26	1.36	0.61
1981	1.32	0.82	8.93	1.25	0.58
1986	1.33	0.68	9.52	1.26	0.51
1991	1.36	0.67	10.08	1.29	0.51
1996	1.37	0.69	10.60	1.30	0.53
2001	1.34	0.70	11.00	1.27	0.54

Source : "Social and Economic Data", Central Statistical Services, Ministry of Treasury, Economics and Intergovernmental Affairs, 1978.

Assessing the Extent of Surplus Space

Figure 3 illustrates the development of school building in Ontario between 1967 and 1976-77 and shows the sizeable public assets which school boards hold in trust. Many boards continued to build even when the decline in enrolments had set in. The reasons were: a certain distrust of forecasts; the need for replacement; and the lack of facilities where new pupil places were needed. As a result, surplus property now has to be disposed of or put to uses for which it was not originally intended.

In the first Information Bulletin issued by CODE the assessment of surplus is based on a comparison between rated capacity and actual enrolments (Figure 4). According to this estimate, the surplus in Ontario amounted in 1977 to 633 090 pupil places. This figure obviously constitutes "gross" surplus since in terms of accommodation surplus is never directly proportionate to the fall in enrolments.

In order to ensure the provision of up-to-date information on actual and projected enrolments the Commission suggests that each board initiates a process whereby projections of "available" surplus can be updated on a yearly basis and related to each school individually. Since occupancy rates vary from board to board, it is recommended that decisions on the use of surplus accommodation should remain a local responsibility. A few examples are given however as to how surplus has been assessed and put to use.

The Toronto Board of Education, one of the pioneers of community use of schools in Ontario, has in recent years developed and implemented guidelines concerning "parallel use of vacant educational space". One of the key policy instruments for making use of surplus accommodation is the establishment of Parallel Use Committees (PUCs) in which local decision-making bodies, school personnel, parents, service groups, businesses and institutions participate. A PUC must be set up whenever a school with less than 700 pupils has a surplus capacity of two or more classrooms and a school with more than 700 pupils four or more surplus classrooms.

Figure 4. **Surplus Capacity in Ontario**

	Rated Capacity (1977)	Enrolment (1976)	Surplus Pupil Places
Public Elementary	1 312 966	929 056	382 110
Secondary	711 293	610 918	100 375
Separate	570 088	420 673	150 605
Total	2 594 347	1 960 647	633 090

Source : The Commission on Declining Enrolments in Ontario, "School Facilities, the Community and Declining Enrolments", *Information Bulletin No. 1,* Toronto, February 1978.

Figure 3. **Ontario School Building Construction, New Schools and Additions, 1967-1976/77**

	Elementary				Secondary				Total			
Year[1]	Enrolment[2] Gain or loss(−)	No. of Projects Completed[3]	New & Replacement Pupil Places	Total Cost at Tender Stage	Enrolment[2] Gain or loss(−)	No. of Projects Completed[3]	New & Replacement Pupil Places	Total Cost at Tender Stage	Enrolment[2] Gain or loss(−)	No. of Projects Completed[3]	New & Replacement Pupil Places	Total Cost at Tender Stage
				$,000's				$,000's				$,000's
1967	40 181	330	72 800	91 117	27 710	108	40 750	133 540	67 891	438	113 550	224 657
1968	25 538	335	77 742	114 417	37 071	56	28 457	101 950	62 609	391	106 199	216 367
1969	25 527	333	67 374	115 395	29 872	56	26 472	93 451	55 399	389	93 846	208 846
1970	9 371	243	74 074	116 832	26 234	65	35 329	117 336	35 605	308	109 403	234 168
1971	−8 648	215	60 486	97 415	17 607	81	28 785	128 231	8 959	296	89 271	225 646
1972	−11 739	221	46 453	88 957	8 493	67	27 287	93 713	−3 246	288	73 740	182 670
1973-74[4]	−22 216	226	36 704	80 721	2 712	64	12 670	48 598	−19 504	290	49 374	129 319
1974-75	−18 046	110	28 864	57 730	3 925	31	8 789	35 772	−14 121	141	37 653	93 502
1975-76	−15 361	163	35 784	88 735	15 510	54	7 404	36 402	149	217	43 188	125 137
1976-77	−29 393	108	25 065	72 554	7 895	25	6 332	35 753	−21 498	133	31 397	108 307
Total	4 786	2 284	525 346	923 873	177 029	607	222 275	824 746	172 243	2 891	747 621	1 748 619

Source : Reports of the Minister of Education.

Use of surplus school accommodation for alternative purposes is also subject to Ministry of Education regulations. Thus, if the ratio of enrolment to related capacity is less than 60 per cent in a school, other boards are entitled to request space ahead of the community.

Figure 5 shows the number of public elementary, public secondary and Roman Catholic Schools (so called separate schools) closed in Ontario between 1970-77. It shows that elementary schools are the first to be closed and that during the last few years of this period a trend towards concentration of elementary schools can be discerned.

Figure 5. **Closings: Number of Schools by Year**

	1970	1971	1972	1973	1974	1975	1976	1977	Total
Elementary	132	115	112	137	29	14	25	33	597
						5[1]	4[1]	49[1]	58
Secondary	11	6	4	5	4	0	0	9	39
					3				3
Separate	27	30	37	41	13	8	8	16	177
								26[1]	26
Total	170	151	153	183	46	22	25	58	813
					3	5	4	75	87

1. Closing after transfer of pupils to other schools.
Source : Reports of the Minister of Education.

Guidelines and suggestions for assessing surplus include:

— The establishment of a long-range master plan covering 10 years;

— Advance planning and research to identify sub-standard and/or inadequate facilities, to study the case of existing facilities and the amount of surplus accommodation in each school;

— Co-operation with neighbouring boards.

Constraints

Ontario school boards faced with surplus generally have the following options: to consolidate their school networks by closing some schools, to twin or pair schools with a view to using surplus for enrichment programmes (Figure 6) or to provide for alternative uses. Community use of schools is often initiated as a result of Community Development Grants from the Ministry of Education.

Neighbourhood residents are becoming increasingly aware of the opportunities offered by surplus school accommodation. They are beginning to regard it as public property to be shared by parents, agencies and organisations for purposes such as legal aid services, clinics, health and psychiatric units, social services, vocational training programmes for the prevention of alcohol and drug addiction, etc. (Figures 7 and 8). The three most common uses today are nurseries, adult day classes and programmes for handicapped children.

The main obstacle to the extension and development of such uses was initially thought to be money, but the real barrier is now considered to be the lack of collaboration on the part of the community at large. Some agencies have therefore started to organise training courses for parents to make these programmes, for which there is a great need, more effective.

As alternative uses are in many instances considered preferable to selling or leasing schools for private, commercial or industrial uses, the state whose task it is to guarantee equal access and the efficient use of public resources, is faced with the problem of the just distribution of resources between municipalities. This problem is linked with the apportioning of the proceeds of sales or leases for alternative community uses and originates in the state-board partnership regulating the financing and acquisition of school properties. It is further exacerbated by the fact that these rules have changed over time, and that such properties are unevenly distributed among municipalities.

To illustrate the emerging problem, two examples are given in the Final Report comparing two boards both of whom are about to sell a surplus school for $1 000 000. It is assumed that the first board acquired its building on the basis of 75 per cent state finance and 25 per cent local finance whereas in the case of the second board only 25 per cent of the costs were financed by the state and the remaining by local arrangements. If the state did not demand a share of the proceeds, the first board would realize a $750 000 benefit, and the second would gain only $250 000. Boards with no surplus properties could make no benefits at all.

The report points out that in the interest of equity the state could demand a "negative grant" from

Figure 6. School in Etobicoke Housing an Alternative High School for Exceptional Students

Figure 7. An Elementary School Wing, now a Juvenile court

Among the alterations: new partitions for smaller offices

Figure 8. A primary School in Etobicoke which now Serves as a Vocational Training Centre

Drawing boards have been installed in former classroom

Mobile food catering replaces the kitchen

The old gym serves as a cafeteria

the first board of $750 000 and from the second of $250 000. However, both boards, especially the first, would then be tempted not to sell but to put their surplus property to some other, less important use. The problems would be "solved" but at the expense of the most effective use of public property.

If, on the other hand, the first board chooses to put its property to an alternative community use, no reimbursement is demanded by the state. The property serves well in its new capacity, i.e. it fulfils a community function. But unless there happens to be comparable properties in each municipality available for community use, the problem of the equitable distribution of resources between municipalities necessarily arises. Inefficient use is also made of a public asset, if a property put to community use does not produce revenues proportionate to its market value.

The Commissioner points out that although the problem of finding equitable and efficient uses for school properties is not a new one, it will take up a more significant part of the school boards' political and administrative tasks in the future. He states:

> The real properties of a board are best viewed as a portfolio of capital assets to be managed in the public interest by the board. As any other portfolio manager, the board must from time to time change the assets of its portfolio and even trade off some of those capital assets to realize cash benefits. In the management of its portfolio, the board will have to seek maximum utility of those assets while conforming to some remarkable constraints associated with the requirements of equity and with the past and present regulations pertaining to the finance of school property acquisitions[3].

While advocating a decentralised and local approach to the management of surplus school space, the Commissioner does not exclude regulations and legislation by the State Ministry of Education to protect the interests of the state taxpayer. He also recommends the exchange of information, skills and experiences to "enable boards to conduct their stewardship of public properties more expertly".

Figure 2 showed that declining school enrolments is but one among many other problems in adjusting public services to changing needs. Among these one of the most crucial is the increasing ratio of pensioners to employed persons which in a few years may make the problem of declining enrolments seem simple. Foreseeing this trend many boards are now beginning to convert surplus school accommodation into apartments for the elderly or meeting places for senior citizens (Figure 9).

Figure 9. **Typical One-bedroom Apartment in Former Classroom**

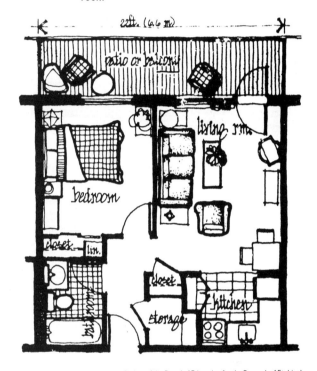

Source: *Project School House,* A Project of the Board of Education for the Borough of Etobicoke, Ontario, 1979.

A second important constraint is the present general recession. Job opportunities have shrunken considerably and structural problems of growth are emerging in Ontario as elsewhere. Education will for some time ahead face hard competition from other public services. In addition, slow improvements in output (and income) per worker, will reduce the increase in public revenues over the foreseeable future. Therefore, it will be difficult enough just to maintain per pupil expenditure at the present real dollar levels and to protect such expenditure from erosion by inflation. The warning issued by the Commissioner that boards should be more cautious in assuming new public service roles must be seen in this overall context.

Current Policies

The present task of Government is twofold in that policies to buffer the effects of declining enrolments on teachers, facilities, programmes, costs and administrative structures must make sense at both state level and local level. In 1969 many small boards were amalgamated into county boards, which were granted greater autonomy. The central level in contrast restricted its influence essentially to issuing recommendations and guidelines. This move towards decentralisation may have to be reviewed in the light of current circumstances.

It is quite conceivable that only counties above a certain size will retain autonomy and that the smaller ones will lose it. (The system does not ressemble that in France or in the United States but like so many features in Canada seems to be a mixture of the two).

The stipulation that local authorities have to prepare long-term, generally 10-year, plans (urban areas have to develop 20-year plans) does not seem in retrospect to have done much to prevent the present crisis situation. Although the Ministry recommended class loadings of 35 pupils, boards usually built for a loading of 32 and actually used classrooms for about 30 pupils.

One of the main recommendations of the Commissioner, therefore, is to increase the role of the state in the planning and use of school properties and to reduce the public debt for school acquisitions. He recommends:

> The Ministry of Education pay in full, from current revenue, the costs of all new sites, buildings and additions, including replacements, approved by the Minister, and hence own them outright. This provision should be made effective as soon as possible and made retroactive to all real property-related expenditures approved after December 31, 1977[4].

In the interest of a more efficient management of public real estate assets the Commissioner suggests:

> Every board be given the authority to dispose of surplus properties and to apply the proceeds immediately to the purchase of other real properties, or to put the proceeds of an escrow account for a period up to five years without the negative grant being imposed. At any time during the five years the board should be allowed to use those funds to purchase new properties, the acquisition of which has been approved by the Ministry. Income from the funds in escrow should be apportioned between the boards and the Ministry in the same proportion as the proceeds from the disposal would have been apportioned[4].

In addition, the Commissioner makes the following recommendations in relation to the present situation:

> A two-year moratorium be placed on building new secondary school accommodations and excess demand for places be accommodated over the short-run by bussing.

> At least 50 per cent of the capital budget be directed to renovation, and these capital funds be paid to the boards on the same basis (i.e. in the same ratio of provincial expenditures to local expenditures) as operating grants.

> Capital expenditures continue to be monitored by the Ministry through regional offices.

> Where surplus capacity of one board can meet the requirements of a neighbouring or overlapping board, the services of the Ministry be offered in negotiating the arrangements and terms, and where it is in the public interest, to mandate these arrangements and terms. The Minister should, if necessary, indicate that ministerial approval of the intended property transactions of both boards is contingent upon such negotiations serving the interests of local and provincial taxpayers.

> All boards be required to prepare for public distribution a statement of their policies and procedures regarding transportation of pupils, possible or anticipated school and classroom closings and the use of space no longer needed for instructional purposes[5].

As a final comment, the Commissioner observes that among the potential economies from declining enrolments are the proceeds accruing from sales or the redeployment of surplus school properties. He points out that the realisation and maximisation of such economies will require a great deal of planning and co-operation on the part of the boards, the Ministry, municipalities and community service agencies.

NOTES

1. *See UNESCO Statistical Yearbook,* 1972, p. 152, and D. Munroe, *The Organisation and Administration of Education in Canada,* Secretariat of State, Education Support Branch, Ottawa, 1974.

2. The Commission on Declining Enrolments in Ontario, Final Report, *op. cit.,* pp. 4-5.

3. *Ibid.,* p. 274.

4. *Ibid.,* p. 278.

5. *Ibid.,* pp. 278-279.

ARLINGTON HEIGHTS, ILLINOIS, UNITED STATES

Identity: Arlington Heights, middle to upper middle class suburban community near Chicago, 75 000 inhabitants, built almost exclusively in the 1950s and 1960s.

Main reasons for surplus space: The aging cycle of the community, birth decline, cost of housing, and land.

Quantity of surplus space: About 60 per cent surplus capacity in terms of pupil places. Five schools have been closed, the rest of the surplus is distributed unevenly throughout the other schools.

Authorities concerned: Four elementary school districts, one high school district, one college district, the local village government.

Most important points: Active involvement of Board of Education to find new users, investigation of community values regarding education in the context of declining enrolments, the establishment of an area-wide committee to study potential uses for closed schools.

Context and Main Reasons for Surplus Space

Arlington Heights has grown from a small suburban community with 1 000 inhabitants in 1950 to an incorporated "village" (comparable to a municipality in other parts of the United States) with 75 000 inhabitants and 10 000 pupils in 1971. Although still largely dependent on Chicago for its economic existence, Arlington Heights has, in the past decades, started to develop its own economic base, as an entity separate from the Chicago metropolitan growth area.

According to 1975 data Arlington Heights population is relatively young (75 per cent are 44 years of age or less); relatively prosperous (less than 2 per cent have an income below poverty level); three-quarters reside in owner occupied dwellings (average value $50 000); the majority is new to the district (60 per cent have lived there for less than 10 years). All in all, the residents of Arlington Heights are a relatively homogeneous group.

Encompassed within Arlington Heights are three public school systems:

— All or parts of four elementary school districts, each with different boundaries and with their own boards and administrative organisations;

— One high school district which maintains three high schools in Arlington Heights and five others in neighbouring communities;

— One college district which supports a community college serving altogether ten villages and townships.

In addition, three private schools run by the church or church-affiliated organisations are available to pupils living in Arlington Heights.

In general, the data and developments discussed in this case study refer to Arlington Heights School District 25, which is the largest of the four elementary school districts.

Within the ten-year period 1965-75 District 25 has experienced both growth and decline of enrolments. Heavy residential construction activity during the 1960s led to an increasing number of families with young children moving into the district. After the children have gone through school, their parents tend to remain in the area. School enrolments thus reached a peak in 1971 with 10 000 pupils and subsequently fell to 6 500 in 1977.

The general decline in birth rates, coupled with a slowdown of construction activity and of the economy in general, have since led to a further reduction in the number of residents and to a continuing fall in school enrolments. The first schools to be affected are those at elementary level. Junior and senior high school enrolments will reach a brief peak and will then follow the same pattern as elementary school enrolments.

Figure 1. **Converted Schools**

Name and Type of School (year built and closed)	New Use	Authority Responsible (funding agency)	Cost of Conversion and Rent/Year (comparable commercial figure based on price for warehouse space $6.00/sq. ft./year) in 1979
1. Dwyer Elementary School (1959-1971)	– Career education – Special education – Illinois Center for Bilingual Education	North West Co-operative (joint projects)	$ 75 000 – conv. $ 45 000 – rent/yr. ($ 100 000 – comp. fig.)
2. North Elementary School (1938-1976)	– Special education	North West Suburban Special Education Organisation	$ 50 000 – conv. $ 174 000 – rent/yr.
3. Wilson Elementary School (1924-1960)	– Summit School for Learning Disabilities – Head Start classes – NEC	– private – NOC – NEC	No cost for conversion $ 37 000 – rent/yr. ($ 220 000 – comp. fig.)
4. Miner Junior High School (1957-1978)	– Junior High School	School District 102	No costs for conversion $ 100 000 – rent/yr. ($ 474 000 – comp. fig.)
5. Belmont Elementary School (1940-1971)	– Center for Instructional Materials Graphic Arts – Center for child and family studies; psychological and social work, parent counselling	High School District 214	Cost for conversion not available $ 7 500 – rent/yr. ($ 85 000 – comp. fig.)

Source : Compiled by the author.

Extent and Consequences of Declining Enrolments

In 1975 Arlington Heights School District 25 employed a group of planning consultants to study the effects of declining enrolments on the school system and the community as a whole. The result was a comprehensive report dealing with fiscal projections and alternative actions to improve resource utilisation[1]. In the report, all schools and their respective catchment areas were studied individually and enrolment projections as well as their consequences discussed. Although the study caused considerable bewilderment in the community in 1975, as projections seemed to be too radical, actual figures today prove that the estimates were rather conservative.

Updated school projections show that by 1984 enrolments in District 25 will be down to 3 716 students (rather than to 5 458 students which was the 1975 consultants' projection). This means a "theoretical" surplus of about 60 per cent of the total number of pupil places available in 1971 to meet the peak of 10 000 pupils. Up to 1978, however, only four elementary and one junior high school have been closed. The rest of the available space is distributed unevenly throughout the remaining schools.

The 1975 report was based on classic cohort survival projections, and it soon proved necessary, in order to provide a more precise base for Board of Education decisions, to introduce an annual updating of these projections incorporating also other local and national data. A pre-school census is made every three to four years. In addition, every principal prepares a forecast for his own school, which offers an additional data base for planning. This is important since the rate of decline varies considerably from one school and one neighbourhood to the next. At the district level projections have been off by 1½ per cent only following the introduction of the annual up-dating mechanism. At the level of the individual school the variance has not exceeded 1 per cent.

One of the important results of the consultants' report was to create a new awareness of the problems associated with declining enrolments. It made the various groups and agencies concerned, including the village government, realise that some action had to be taken in respect of facilities, personnel and financing.

When the report was issued, the Board of Education conducted a series of nine public meetings involving more than 1 000 people. At the end of each meeting, the Board solicited public input concerning the educational value structure the community wished to preserve. Based on the community's response, a long-range planning proposal was issued stating the trade-off decisions which the Board had to take to achieve a balance between the neighbourhood school concept, breadth of programme and school closings taking into account fiscal, administrative as well as social aspects[2].

One of the priority requests of the community concerned the maintenance of the neighbourhood school, whereas the main preoccupation of the Board of Education was to keep as many options open as possible for future boards to enable them to respond to declining as well as increasing enrolments.

School closures were also discussed and were seen to be essentially an organisational problem. The split in age groups between the elementary school (grades 1-5), the junior high or middle school (grades 6-8) and the senior high school (grades 9-12), established during the period of increasing enrolments was put under close scrutiny. Summarising the findings of nineteen research studies on this topic, the Educational Research Service, which acted as consultant to Arlington Heights' Board of Education, concluded that there was no consistently favourable rationale for either the existing structure or for the more conventional elementary (1-6 grades)/high school (7-12 grades) organisation. One of the less disruptive and most flexible ways of reorganising the school network proved to be to close some junior high schools, to consolidate others and, where appropriate, to transfer the 6th grade to the elementary school.

Besides the organisational problem and cost considerations there are a number of other factors that need to be taken into account. Among these is the difficulty of converting elementary schools which, in accordance with the neighbourhood school concept. have been built in the midst of residential areas. Any non-residential use of such schools will result in increased traffic and noise and also in other inconveniences for the neighbourhood.

Criteria for the Redeployment of Resources

Arlington Heights is one of the few cases which offers the possibility of comparing two distinct approaches to redeployment: the school district's and the village government's. While the school district is concerned with educational criteria (structure of the education system, accessibility, suitability of building) and with costs, essentially personnel costs (Figure 2), the village government is more interested in making optimum use of outdoor areas and building resources to improve the physical infrastructure of the community for purposes such as recreation and social services. It argues for the conversion of spacious school grounds into parks and investigates the potential of closed schools in terms of reuse for other than educational purposes.

In an analysis of the schools closed or proposed for closing the Planning Department of the village of Arlington Heights states:

> Faced with declining enrolments and rising educational costs, Arlington Heights School District No. 25 has found it necessary to close two of its elementary schools (actually 3), North School and Wilson School, and one of its junior high schools, either Thomas or Miner School.

> After much consideration and discussion the School District No. 25 Board of Education decided to close Miner Junior High.

> The school buildings on these four sites represent an investment of approximately $12 000 000 made by the residents of Arlington Heights. Any change in the use of these four school sites will have an impact on the neighbourhoods in which these schools are located. In the light of these facts, James T. Ryan, Arlington Heights Village President, requested the Village Planning Department to prepare a planning analysis of the four schools in District No. 25 which are closed or proposed for closing[3].

The criteria according to which the village government analyses the school sites differ considerably from those of the Board of Education. They include building deficiencies, loading docks, lighting, screening, landscaping, etc. (Figure 3).

Figure 2. **Declining Enrollment Fact Sheet**

FINANCIAL SUMMARY

It is estimated, based on early projections, that "if" the state fully funds the formula next year the district will be able to balance budgets as forecasted previously and announced during the last referendum. However, even if the district is able to slightly reduce warrants in 1977-78 due to some temporary cash flow advantage and thus reduce carry-forward debt in 1978-79, there still appears to be a probable deficit of almost $500 000 in the 1978-79 budget, even with a return to full current borrowing levels on both old and new local tax rate incomes. This appears consistent with prior forecasts and with the general trends projected by Booz, Allen and Hamilton.

ENROLLMENT PROJECTIONS

COMPARISON OF "MOST LIKELY" ENROLLMENTS OF ORIGINAL BOOZ, ALLEN AND HAMILTON PROJECTIONS,
1975 UPDATED PROJECTIONS AND CURRENT 1976 PROJECTIONS

	1975	1976	1977	1978	1979	1980	1981	1982	1983	1984	1985	1986
B., A. & H. Projections												
K-5	4 938	4 767	4 569	4 349	4 195	4 078	3 903	3 724	3 609	3 502		
6-8	3 000	2 812	2 673	2 517	2 408	2 291	2 216	2 165	2 093	1 956		
Total	7 938	7 579	7 242	6 866	6 603	6 369	6 119	5 889	5 702	5 458		
1975 Projections												
K-5		4 731	4 557	4 287	4 173	4 037	3 865	3 689	3 576	3 472	3 328	
6-8		2 790	2 641	2 568	2 419	2 342	2 197	2 181	2 088	1 954	1 867	
Total		7 521	7 198	6 855	6 592	6 379	6 062	5 870	5 664	5 426	5 195	
1976 Projections												
K-5			4 275	3 939	3 763	3 539	3 276	3 106	2 977	2 855	2 699	2 564
6-8			2 578	2 451	2 279	2 183	2 068	1 971	1 814	1 615	1 543	1 490
Total			6 853	6 390	6 042	5 722	5 344	5 077	4 791	4 470	4 242	4 054

ESTIMATED 1977-78 SAVINGS RESULTING FROM DECLINING ENROLLMENT

With the projected enrollment decline of 438 students, it is estimated that the certificated staff will be decreased by fourteen positions resulting in savings of $154 000. These savings are reflected in the financial summary above.

ESTIMATED SAVINGS ASSOCIATED WITH THE CLOSING OF ONE ELEMENTARY SCHOOL

Reduction of 14 certified staff		
Reduction of additional 3 certified staff, 3 classified staff and other building related savings	$80 650	
Student transportation savings	0 to 8 500	$80 650 to $89 150

ESTIMATED SAVINGS ASSOCIATED WITH THE CLOSING OF ONE JUNIOR HIGH SCHOOL

Reduction of 14 certified staff	178 050	
Reduction of additional 7 certified staff, 6 classified staff and other building related savings		
Student transportation increased costs[1]	0 to 22 500	$155 550 to $178 050

ESTIMATED SAVINGS ASSOCIATED WITH THE CLOSING OF ONE ELEMENTARY SCHOOL AND ONE JUNIOR HIGH SCHOOL

Reduction of 14 certified staff	178 050	
Reduction of additional 7 certified staff, 6 classified staff and other junior high related savings		
Reduction of additional 3 certified staff, 3 classified staff and other elementary related savings	80 650	
Student transportation increased costs[1]	8 500 to 22 500	$236 200 to $267 200

ESTIMATED SAVINGS ASSOCIATED WITH THE CLOSING OF TWO JUNIOR HIGH SCHOOLS

Reduction of 14 certified staff	372 100	
Reduction of additional 21 certified staff, 12 classified staff and other building related savings		
Student transportation increased costs[2]	2 500 to 22 500	$349 600 to $369 600

1. These figures vary depending on which junior high school is closed. Based on the possible boundaries described herein the followings ranges of transportation cost increases would apply: Close Miner – $0; close Rand – $2 500 to $7 500; close South – $7 500 to $22 500; close Thomas – $5 000 to $10 000. These are net costs and reflect state reimbursement to be received in fiscal year 1978.
2. The junior high school combinations remaining open would alter additional transportation costs as follows: Close Miner and Rand – $2 500 to $7 500; close South and Rand – $10 000 to $15 000; close Thomas and Miner – $15 000 to $20 000; close Thomas and South – $17 500 to $22 500. These are also net costs reflecting state reimbursement.
Source: Arlington Heights Planning Department, "Analysis of the Schools Closed or Proposed for Closing", Arlington Heights, Illinois, September 8, 1977.

Figure 3. **Planning Department Analysis of the Schools Closed or Proposed for Closing**

BUILDING	North	Wilson	Miner	Thomas
Year of Original Construction	1938	1934	1957	1964
Additions Constructed In:	1949	1938-56-9	1961-64	1966
Land Area	2.7 A	4.9 A	11.5 A	13.0 A
Total Building Floor Area	29 000 sf	37 000 sf	82 000 sf	86 000 sf
Number of Floors	2	2	2	2
Serious Building Deficiencies				
Conversion Impossible				
Loading Dock Unavailable	•	•		•
Building Should Be Removed				
SITE				
Inadequate Outdoor Lighting	•	•		•
Inadequate Perimeter Screening	•	•	•	•
Inadequately Fenced				
Inadequate Landscaping	•	•		•
Poor Site Aesthetics				
No Accommodations for Additional Parking				
Internal Traffic Unsatisfactory	•			
Ingress and Egress Problems				
Inadequate Setbacks			•	
Fire Safety Problems[1]	N.A.	N.A.	N.A.	N.A.
Improper Garbage Storage	•	•		
Site Expansion Impractical		•	•	•
Adverse Effect on Adjoining Residential Properties				
Inadequate Public Utilities				
Water Retention Problems				
Inadequate Public Improvements	•			
TRAFFIC				
Minor Traffic Problems	•	•	•	•
Serious Traffic Problems				
Serious Pedestrian Hazards				
Public Transportation Unavailable			•	•

1. Information unavailable from Village and State Fire Marshals.
NA   Non Available.
Source :   See Figure 2.

In contrast, the Board of Education long range planning report — besides organisational, personnel and cost considerations — places more emphasis on community values in relation to education. Following the hearings and meetings conducted by the Board in 1975, these values were summarised as follows according to order of importance:

Quality of Education. Defined as achieving excellence in those programmes either mandated or at district option. This is characterized in part by determination of desired class size and supporting staff levels.

Neighborhood Schools. Desirability of maintaining elementary (K through 5 or 6) schools in geographic locations which permit children to walk to school, involve the parents and school staff in the educational process, and avoid overcrowding in the classrooms.

Breadth of Programmes. The desire of the community to include the fine arts (music and art), industrial arts, home-making, physical education, etc., in the educational curriculum along with the traditional and mandated classroom subjects and special education.

Bussing. Bussing of elementary children obviously conflicts with the high order value of the neighborhood school for younger children. Bussing of junior high children was acceptable if adequate safety precautions were observed[4].

Taking into account the value structure outlined above, additional management data and further public input, and following extensive discussions at the administrative level, the actions taken included:

— Major reductions in staff, materials, services and programmes;

— An active search for alternative educational or other compatible programmes to fill empty spaces;

— The closing of two elementary schools and one junior high school; and

— A tax referendum which was passed in May 1976.

In 1977, all school districts and Boards of Education as well as parent representatives, village trustees and municipal departments formed a "Committee to Study Potential Uses for Closed Schools". The first meeting of the committee held in November 1977 revealed that surplus school space had become an entry point for co-ordination between all parties concerned.

The Committee defined its task as follows: "To provide a forum with advisory capacity to help each body involved to make better decisions". In February 1978, the Committee issued its report on School Closings[5]. The report deals with the causes of declining enrolments and with legal aspects of and procedures for closing schools. The Committee recommends that the following criteria, which combine educational considerations with community interests, should be applied to assess the need for school closings:

— Quality of program;

— Maintain neighborhood schools where possible;

— Breadth of program;

— Cost implications, including transportations;

— Alternate uses;

— Modernization potential;

— Building capacity;

— Traffic and safety considerations;

— Quality of life;

— Distribution of population, present and future;

— Other factors deemed appropriate.

Each case of school closure and alternative use has been decided individually on the basis of compatibility with land use patterns, cost/revenue considerations and implications for future use. There seems to be general agreement on the following order of priorities for reuse:

— Educational uses;

— Other public uses;

— Other desirable private uses;

— Sale or disposal.

A three-year "softening policy" related to the decrease of state funds for education as a result of declining enrolments helps the district to adjust to the new situation. This is a special measure of the Illinois State Board of Education, which does not exist in every state. While it is being recognized by local boards as a useful policy, federal incentives for the conversion of surplus school space for community uses, as proposed for instance in the so-called Heinz Bill[6], are likely to have but limited impact on local decisions since they provide "seed money" only and the local taxpayer, as a rule, has to carry subsequent running costs.

Demand for Surplus Space and Types of Reuse

The demand for space can best be measured by looking at the type and extent of reuse made of empty school facilities. As is often the case, there are no statistics available regarding unmet needs for space. Educational and community needs have absorbed most of Arlington Heights' surplus school accommodation: day-care, pre-school, special education, bilingual education, adult and further education are now well-established programmes which still continue to grow.

No school has been converted into housing as for instance in Massachusetts or for industrial use as in Michigan. One school has been on the market for sale but did not attract a high enough bid. The sale was subsequently postponed since real estate appraisals showed that due to a new underpath the value of the property was going up. The school now serves for adult education and training programmes.

The first type of "legitimate" uses for surplus space relates to improved provision ("this is where we should have been all along"). For example, full-time music and arts rooms are now the rule rather than the exception in every school. Four or five rooms in another school have been used to create a teacher centre for in service training and curriculum development. It effectively integrates what was previously a scattered activity and improves the educational service. This would not have been possible without surplus space.

A second type of use is illustrated by North School, now fully occupied by the North West Suburban Special Education Organization, which serves High School Districts No. 211 and No. 214 and various elementary school districts in and around Arlington Heights. The Organization is governed by a joint agreement and its aim is to help the physically handicapped, deaf or otherwise disabled child develop to his/her fullest potential. Each school district is responsible for running its own special education classes and for hiring and paying the teachers needed for these. All districts share administrative costs, facilities and equipment.

In a subsequent phase, surplus space has been used to meet social needs or a combination of social and educational needs. An example is the volunteer service bureau which serves school and community members alike. It co-ordinates 1 800 volunteers who give an average of 200 hours per year or 3-4 hours per week to various causes at the request of teachers or private individuals. Another example is the Summit School for Learning Disabilities and Head Start Classes established in Wilson School (Figures 4 and 5).

In most cases, the cost of conversion has been borne by the new user. Outlays for conversion usually remain rather low: new partitions, new lighting, new paint, some special provisions and equipment are often the only additions to the existing buildings.

Concluding Remarks

Arlington Heights is an example of a community which actively deals with the problem of declining enrolments. The quality of the solutions found are to a large extent dependent on:

— The personality of the Superintendant and his readiness to deal with the challenge of surplus school accommodation;

— The extent of community awareness and the active involvement of local government;

— The early input of expert advice which helped to activate agencies and user groups and to co-ordinate their views.

Figure 4. Recreation Area in the Summit School for Learning Disabilities

Figure 5. Head Start Classes in Wilson School

Pre-school classes aiming at preparing children from disadvantaged families for school

The scarce public attendance at the first committee meeting in November 1977 to study potential uses for closed schools may simply indicate that the whole issue of closing and reusing schools was not perceived as a threatening problem by most community members. The meeting showed, however, the complexity of finding appropriate solutions in a highly decentralised and fragmented, yet independent, system of government.

By 1979, Arlington Heights had accepted declining enrolments and empty schools as part of its overall development. All surplus space was occupied by new users and some changes of use had already occured since 1977. Because of the openness in publishing projection data and soliciting community input through public meetings and advisory committees[7], no further conflicts had arisen between the Board of Education and the community concerning the closing or reuse of schools.

When comparing the rents received for leased surplus schools with those paid for even the cheapest storage space (see Figure 1), it is clear that the price of maintaining the neighbourhood school concept is extremely high. If schools had not been built in the midst of residential areas but located, for instance, near commercial centres, the chances would have been greater of finding users who could pay adequate rents. On the other hand,

this might have meant that certain community needs would have remained unsatisfied.

Compared to the cost of mothballing a school, however, even a small amount of rent can be considered a profit. Thus, the Arlington Board of Education regards itself to be $31 000 better off in the case of a school bringing a net revenue of $13 000 a year and for which the annual cost of mothballing is estimated at $18 000. This seems to be a realistic way of looking at the cost aspects.

Finally, if the extent of declining enrolments and resources could have been predicted ten or fifteen years ago, the provision of educational facilities in Arlington Heights would probably have differed in four main respects:

— Campus type school sites grouping elementary schools, junior and senior high schools would have been preferred to individual sites in order to provide more flexibility for adjusting to peaks and troughs in enrolments;

— Schools would have been zoned off from residential areas;

— Fewer and larger elementary schools, each with a capacity of about 600 to 700 pupils would have been built instead of the great number of small neighbourhood schools; and

— A greater effort would have been made to design schools for energy savings.

NOTES

1. Allen, Booz and Hamilton, "Final Report Arlington Heights District 25: Study of Enrolments and Fiscal Projections, and Alternative Actions to Improve Resource Utilization", Chicago, November 20, 1975.

2. Arlington Heights Public Schools, School District 25, "School Board Rules and Regulations: Long Range Planning", Arlington Heights, Illinois, March 23, 1976.

3. Arlington Heights Planning Department, "Analysis of the Schools Closed or Proposed for Closing", Arlington Heights, Illinois, September 8, 1977.

4. Arlington Heights Public Schools, School District 25, "School Board Rules and Regulations: Long Range Planning", op. cit., pp. 1-2.

5. Arlington Heights, Committee on Closed Schools, "Schools Closing Committee Report", Arlington Heights, Illinois, February 1978.

6. U.S. Congress, Committee on Banking, Housing and Urban Affairs, 95th Congress, 1st Session, SD 792, op. cit.

7. Arlington Heights Elementary School District, "District 25 studies future — Phase II study to begin", in Newsletter, February 1979.

SOLLEFTEÅ, SWEDEN

Identity: Sollefteå is a small rural municipality with 26 000 inhabitants in the northern parts of Sweden.

Main reasons for surplus space: Economic decline of the area and outmigration of the young and childbearing age groups.

Quantity of surplus space: About 60 per cent of all schools have been closed. The rest is often heavily underused.

Authorities concerned: The local school board, Kommunförbundet (National Association of Municipalities) and the National Board of Education.

Most important points: Social and political reasons for not accepting early population forecasts indicating surplus, emphasis on industrial reuse of schools for economic reasons, low-cost alternative uses of empty schools for recreational and community purposes.

Context and Main Reasons for Surplus Space

In Sweden as a whole the problems caused by changing school populations are considerable but in rural areas they are simply staggering, This is particularly true for the northern parts of the country where these problems are exacerbated by economic decline. The Sollefteå area is no exception in this respect.

For a long time, the economic base of the area was the construction of large dams and hydroelectric power plants, wood pulp factories, forestry and agriculture. All these sectors have experienced drastic decline since the early 70s. Between 1944 and 1978 twenty-two dams and hydroelectric power plants were built in the area (Figure 1). No more projects of this size are being planned. Because of international competition the wood pulp industry has considerably reduced its activity: of the twenty-two factories which existed in the area only two remain in operation today. The once fairly labour-intensive forest industry has been largely mechanized and the small or medium-sized farms in the area suffered a severe setback following a decision by the Government in 1968 to promote structural changes in agriculture by subsidizing only larger farms.

These developments in combination have led to a considerable migration from the area of the young and productive age groups and an aging of the population remaining in the area. From a relatively stable population of about 40 000 between 1920 and 1948, the number of inhabitants has since fallen steadily, and in 1977 was only 26 000. All forecasts predict a further reduction. In 1967, the Sollefteå school system served about 5 000 pupils whereas the corresponding figure for 1977 was 3 500. All types of schools were affected.

Besides having to adjust to the general decrease in school population, in itself an almost impossible task, the Sollefteå school administration had to face a number of additional problems. These all tended to further increase the amount of surplus school accommodation.

First among these problems was the continuous shift of people following the construction of hydroelectric power plants. Thus, it is interesting to note that the location of the schools (Figure 2) closely matches that of the power plants (Figure 1). However, the quantitative assumptions behind the decision to build often proved to be unfounded, sometimes soon after the completion of a new school.

A second problem which has greatly contributed to the existing surplus is one of inaccuracy of forecasts or unwillingness to accept forecasts, as the following two examples show. A forecast made in Näsåker (now part of Sollefteå) indicated a need for 24 classrooms; in retrospect, it turned out that 3 would have been enough. In contrast, the 1970 forecast by a far-sighted school administrator clearly showed the steady decline of the area and demonstrated that the secondary school planned in Sollefteå was not only overdimensioned but in fact superfluous since pupils could be bussed to schools with spare capacity in neighbouring districts. This was considered politically unacceptable — no politician at the time was ready to discuss openly the consequences of population decline — and the school was built.

A third group of factors contributing to creating surplus is linked to central/local government relationships, national educational reforms, changing standards for schools and a national grant system which favoured the building of new schools and discouraged the renovation and remodelling of old schools. It also often proved difficult for Central Government to assess whether applications from local authorities for new schools were justified or not. There was also a trend at one time in the Sollefteå area to use school building as a way to boost the construction industry.

Finally, a major administrative reform in 1970-71 led to the incorporation of ten municipalities into Sollefteå to form one new municipality. This move was followed by a restructuring of the school network in the district to eliminate underused schools.

Assessing the Extent of Surplus Space

The exact amount of surplus school accommodation has been difficult to assess, mainly due to the lack of data and exact records. A first survey quoted in 1976 by the local school board showed that out of 52 schools 29 were used for other purposes and only 23 served their original purpose. A second survey was carried out by a joint group of interested administrators from the municipality and the local school board in 1977 for the purpose of this study. It can be assumed that this survey provides a reasonably exact record of the actual number of schools built in the area between 1900 and 1977. Instead of the 29 schools first mentioned, the second survey lists 45 schools which have been given over to other uses (Figure 3).

There are economic reasons for not disclosing the exact amount of surplus school accommodation, for example, the fear of having to repay Central Government if a school is used for other purposes, or of losing financial support for new building projects if the amount of existing surplus becomes known. At the time this report was written, the grants requested from Central Government were far in excess of available financial resources. Since then, funds for school building have been even further reduced.

A number of educational reasons also exist for not wanting to assess the exact extent of surplus space. There is uncertainty about the implications for space requirements of the 1976 Bill on New Working Conditions in Schools, known as the SIA (Skolans Inre Arbete) reform. Closely linked to this is the need to improve the quality of provision in many existing schools, e.g. for practical subjects or social activities. In addition, a number of new

Figure 1. Hydroelectric Power Plants Built in the Sollefteå Area between 1944 and 1978

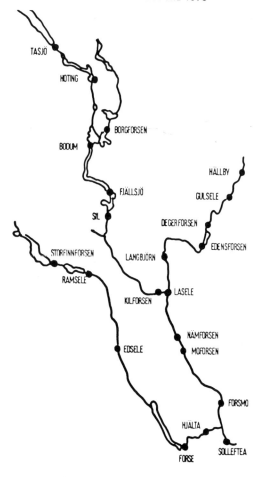

Source: Based on material submitted by the Municipality of Sollefteå.

Figure 2. Location of Schools in the Sollefteå Area

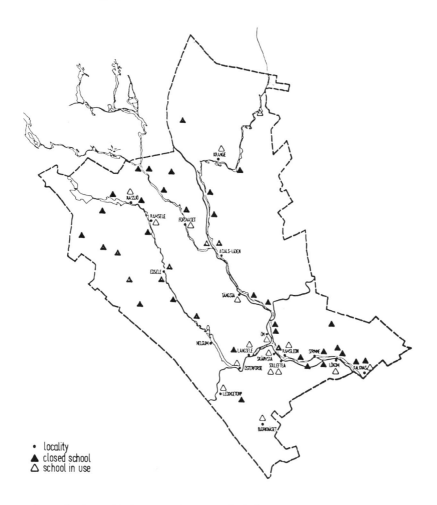

- locality
▲ closed school
△ school in use

Source: Based on material submitted by the Municipality of Solleftea?.

educational needs are emerging in areas such as pre-primary education, vocational training, adult education, retraining courses, teacher training etc.

Finally, there are also institutional and organisational arrangements which make it difficult to assess the extent of surplus, for example, the division of work and responsibility between the local school board and the municipal building or real estate office. Once a school building has been handed over for other than educational uses, it disappears from the records of the school board and is to be found in the records of the municipality under the use made of it (factory, community centre, etc.).

In almost all cases, lack of pupils has been the basis for declaring a school surplus. The dispersed settlement pattern and the financial and social costs of bussing children over long distances have often made the decision to close a difficult one. In some cases, therefore, schools with only 14 pupils (e.g. Forsnäs) have been kept open. In one exceptional case, a perfectly good school working to full capacity had to be closed because it proved impossible to adapt it to accommodate handicapped pupils, in accordance with recent regulations.

The Sollefteå School Board keeps simple records of all its schools with indications of current enrolments and potential new entrants in the next seven years (Figure 4). These records are now up-dated every year since the previous five-year forecasts proved insufficient as a basis for decision-making.

In addition, a number of quick studies have been undertaken to determine which schools should be

Figure 3. Closed Schools and New Uses According to 1977 Survey

No.	Name	Year built	Year closed	No. of classrooms	m²	Current use					Current owner	
						Housing	Industry	Association	Community	Other	Community	Private
1	Bäckdalsskolan	1954	1971	3	900		X				X	
2	Tjällsskola	1952	1969	3			X		X		X	
3	Multra	1948	1968	3				X	X		X	
4	Remsle gamla skola	~1910	1956	2	355			X			X	
5	Myre	1957	1967	2	345	X					X	
6	Ed 1	~1900	~1965	1	160	X			X		X	
7	Ed 2	~1900	1973	3		X						X
8	Bodvill	~1920	~1965	3		X						X
9	Valviken	1928	1967	6	400			X			X	
10	Viksmon	1917	1960	2	167	X		X			X	
11	Holmstrand	1963	1970	6	348			X			X	
12	Nyland	~1890	~1950	2		X		X			X	
13	Garlehöjden	1938 reb.[1] 1953	1965	2	228	X		X			X	
14	Gulsele	1930 reb. 1953	1972	2	228	X		X			X	
15	Junselevallen	1943 reb. 1957 reb. 1963	1969	4	700			X			X	
16	Holafors	~1920	~1965	2		X		X			X	
17	Asmon	1953	1969	4			X				X	
18	Ra	?	?									X
19	Vimmervattnet	?	?									X
20	Vallen, Ramsele	1924	1964									X
21	Flyn	1918	1964	2		X						X
22	Nässjö	–	–			X						X
23	Västvattnet	–	–			X						X
24	Rensjön	–	–			X						X
25	Lungsjön	1930 reb. 1953	1975	4	600			X	X		X	
26	Nordantjäl	1952	1971	4	650		X	X			X	
27	Meafors	–	–									X
28	Lillterrsjö	1923	1962	2		X						X
29	Imnäs	1953	1969	6	800		X	X			X	
30	Ovanmo	1925	1964	~2		X						X
31	Ramnea	–	–					X				X
32	Nordanaker	–	–			X						X
33	Fjällbohög	1932	1960	~2		X						X
34	Vägersjö	1930	1969	~2				X				X
35	Gideaberg	1921	1961	~6				X				X
36	Strandmon	–	–			X						X
37	Stenviksstrand	–	–			X						X
38	Para g:a skola	1910	1949	2	144	X						X
39	Björka smaskola	~1920	~1955	1	180	X						X
40	Björka folksola	1920	~1955	2	286					X	X	
41	Björksjön	1920	1964	2	150	X						X
42	Grillom	–	1956	2	195					X		X
43	Offer	–	1962	3	290	X	X					X
44	Gardnås	~1940	1962	2	150			X				X
45	Eden	~1890	~1950	~2				X				X

1. reb. = rebuilt.
2. ~ = approximately.
Source: Information provided by the Municipality of Sollefteå.

phased out and which should be consolidated, what the structural conditions of the schools are and how employment opportunities and settlement patterns relate to school locations. One study investigates priorities and attitudes towards education among school council members and the population at large.

Figure 4. **Record of Schools and School population
in the Municipality of Sollefteå**

Sollefteå schools listed in alphabetical order. For each school a table indicates enrolments by grade on 1st January (in this example 1976) and under the heading "below age", "0" corresponds to estimated new entrants the following autumn (in this case 1976), "−1" to new entrants the year after (i.e. in the autumn of 1977) etc.

BILLSTA

The school was built in 1962. Two-entry junior level school (grades 1-3).

Present enrolments by grade									Below age						
9	8	7	6	5	4	3	2	1	0	−1	−2	−3	−4	−5	−6
Valla			Lillänget			128	109	101	112	94	115	113	108	109	116

The potential school population under the heading "below age" covers not only Billsta school but also the schools in Lillänget and Skärvsta.

BJÖRKNÄSET

The school was built around 1920 and rebuilt in 1954. Multi-grade teaching at junior and middle levels (grades 1-3 and 4-6) shared with Ledinge school through bussing.

Present enrolments by grade									Below age						
9	8	7	6	5	4	3	2	1	0	−1	−2	−3	−4	−5	−6
Långsele			14	8	9	6	8	4	3	7	1	7	12	8	3

Source : Sollefteå kommun, *Skolor och Elevunderlag*, Sollefteå, 1976.

Using Surplus Space

Schools in Sweden have always been open for community and recreational uses after school hours. Therefore, shared use of parts of a school, i.e. empty classrooms, for such purposes is not uncommon. In general, however, the school administration prefers to consolidate schools. i.e. restructure the network, and hand over redundant schools to the municipality for other community uses or sale, unless they are likely to be needed again for educational purposes.

Of the 45 schools closed only 19 are still owned by the municipality, all others have been sold to private owners; 23 have become permanent dwellings or summer houses (Figure 5); 18 are used by different associations, often sports clubs (Figure 6); 4 for other community purposes (Figure 7); 6 by industry (Figures 8 and 9); and 2 for other purposes (e.g. storage space or warehouse). In a number of cases the buildings are used for double purposes such as associations and other community uses or industry and associations. In nearly all cases, the former teacher flat is owned or inhabited by families who look after the building if it is used for public purposes. Generally, industrial use has been made of the more solid stone buildings while wooden buildings have been sold as private houses or are used for recreation or social purposes. Figures 5 to 8 clearly show that most schools have been converted to their new uses with little structural changes and capital costs. In the majority of cases, the users are quite satisfied with the accommodation.

Figure 5. Ed School

The School built around 1900 and phased out in 1973, has been converted into apartments

Figure 6. The School in Viksmon

The school built in 1917 and closed in 1960, has been converted to accommodate, besides
one apartment, a gymnasium and a meeting room for the local ski and football clubs

Figure 7. Multrå Church and Community Centre

The school next to the church was built in 1948 and closed in 1968.
The municipality owns the building and pays for its maintenance. The Church provides the looms and a meeting room, a pottery workshop
in the basement operates on a commercial basis. Discussions have been initiated to recover the school for its original purpose to meet the
needs of a new nearby housing area

Figure 8. Bäckdal School

The school, built in 1954 and closed in 1971, now serves as a lamp store on the first floor and as a machine and welding shop on the ground floor (this is the second temporary use after the departure of a trailer company). Changes include new curtains, carpeting and partitions for smaller offices

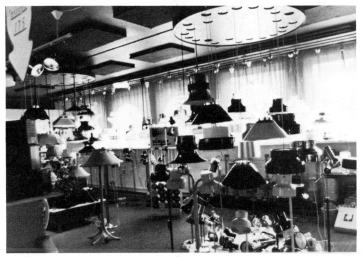

Figure 9. **The School in Åsmon**

The school built in 1953 and closed in 1969, originally accommodated 150 pupils.
It now houses a government training programme for mechanics. Structural change include new steel supports for
heavy machines, crane fixtures, larger doors, acoustic insulation panels, ventilation and new electric power plugs.
Offices are located in the former teacher apartment annex

Current Policies and Future Prospects

During the initial phase of decline following the mid-50s school closures did not meet with any resistance from the population. However, in recent years it has become clear that parents are no longer willing to accept decisions by authorities without being consulted. In one case the community forced the school board to reopen a school and converted the empty part of the school into a community centre. In a second case, the community was reluctant to return a school building, which had been used for two years as a community centre, to the school board for educational use. Discussions were initiated between the municipality who owned the building, the community who used it and the school board to determine how much of the present community centre would be needed to accommodate the school population from a new housing area in the neighbourhood.

As a result of these incidents, two policy changes were introduced: namely to involve the community in the decision-making process and to maintain a school as long as possible within the school system.

At the national level there is a trend away from nation-wide educational reforms and standards towards greater local and regional autonomy in educational matters. When this report was written, Central Government faced the following dilemma (which may since have disappeared with growing decentralisation): if it subsidized those areas most in need of new schools, it encouraged migration to the south; if it invested in school buildings in the north, it ran the risk of satisfying short-term needs which could possibly have been solved by other means or needs that did not really exist. In the past, school construction was often used as a means of creating or attracting employment and showing political support to economically declining rural areas. At present a tight budgetary situation no longer allows funds to be "wasted" in this way.

In the 1950s the one-room school house was no longer considered educationally viable and small schools were abandoned in favour of large central schools often covering grades 1-9 inclusive. Subsequently, the new curriculum introduced in the late 1960s and providing an increasing number of options in grades 7-9, necessitated an even larger pupil base. This led to further inter-municipal co-operation to create central schools for this level in which children could be educated according to the new standards. This educational movement was one of the reasons for the municipal reforms starting in 1971 and gathering momentum in 1974. Today, the development tends to go in the opposite direction. Schools are increasingly considered to be too large and impersonal and there is now discussion about dividing municipalities into smaller units and larger schools into "family groups". These multi-age groups would in fact be rather similar to those which existed in the one-room school house. But the situation has changed in terms of teacher education, family expectations and settlement patterns and a return to the very small school is most unlikely.

However, in view of these continuous changes the school board's current policy to hold on to schools for as long as possible seems understandable. Local decision-makers consider that it would be an advantage if the co-operation and co-ordination between the board and the municipal real estate office could be further developed.

The larger number of redundant schools in the Sollefteå area is but one facet of a whole complex of problems. These affect other societal sectors even more deeply and raise questions about cultural, political and economic values and decision-making processes. To bring about new and brighter prospects for the area would demand a concerted effort to tackle all problems.

At the moment every element of the social and technical infrastructure seems overdimensioned. There are too many empty houses, too many empty schools and roads, too many empty factories and too many people without work.

The first priority of the local decision-makers is to attract new industry. All empty schools built of bricks and stone are therefore presented first to industrial users, often for very little money. Attracting industry to the area is a difficult task and nobody seems to believe that this part of the country will be revitalized without massive governmental grants. On the other hand, there is a new trend for young people to move back into the area, often to work on their parents farm. However, nobody is able to predict whether this is just a temporary or permanent phenomenon.

Identity: Inner London is the central area of the capital; it is an urban area with high population density (approximately 2.5 million inhabitants on 12 000 hectares — more than 200 persons per residential hectare).

Main reasons for surplus space: Combined effects of decentralisation policies (development of sub-urbanisation and new towns), urban decay, falling birth rates and obsolete schools.

Quantity of surplus space: Only a minority of schools have been closed. Most schools have taken the opportunity to improve standards of educational provision or have been used to introduce other forms of education.

Authorities concerned: Inner London Education Authority (ILEA), administering the educational affairs of 13 boroughs in Central London and catering for approximately 95 per cent of all pupils of this area (the rest being educated in private schools).

Most important points: Uneven distribution of surplus and shortages, computerised system to assess educational needs and to evaluate the existing stock, numerous examples of redeployment for educational, social or recreational purposes.

Context and Main Reasons for Surplus Space

England experienced the combined effects of industrialisation and urbanisation earlier than other European countries. London in particular has suffered from these effects which were exacerbated by its administrative and governmental functions.

The late 19th century saw the beginning of urban sprawl: city planners tried to improve the situation by building suburbs which were linked with the city centre by rail transport (Figure 1). But even after World War II the aim to relieve overcrowding had not been achieved. Therefore a number of new towns were created at a reasonable distance from London to provide housing and new jobs. As a result, Inner London suffered severe losses of jobs. Especially skilled people and professional workers moved to the new towns.

The population of Inner London dropped significantly, from 3.2 million in 1961 to 2.77 million in 1971 and less than 2.5 million in 1978. Birth rates dropped simultaneously. Only the 1978 figures indicate slight increasing birth rates but no one expects them to reach the levels experienced in the sixties (Figure 2). Current births show a high percentage of children of immigrant families. Total primary school population fell from over 200 000 in 1965 to less than 150 000 in 1979. ILEA estimates indicate a further fall to less than 125 000 by 1983, to be followed by a period of relatively stable school populations until 1990 (Figure 3).

Although demographic reasons have played a major part in the emergence of surplus school accommodation in Inner London, there are a number of other reasons too:

— The reorganisation of secondary education on comprehensive lines leaving a residue of old school buildings;

— School accommodation unfit to serve modern educational requirements (especially upper floors in 3-decker nursery and primary schools considered by the Plowden report to be substandard);

— Limited site standards of many inner city schools inhibiting outdoor activities or necessary extensions;

— Buildings too small to introduce 3- or 4-form entry schools regarded as a minimum for secondary education (however, recently, two or more small schools were used to form a "dispersed secondary school").

Figure 1.   The Growth of London and Ratio of Persons to Residential Land, 1972

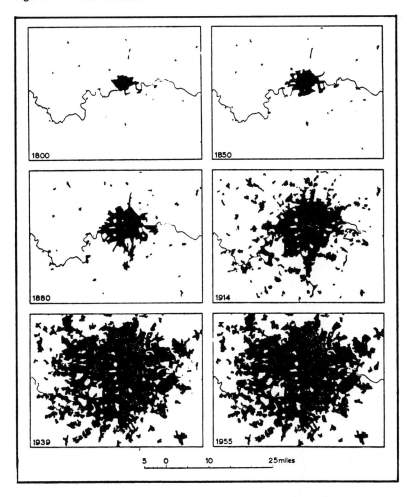

Source: Carter, Harold, *The Study of Urban Geography*, London, 1972.

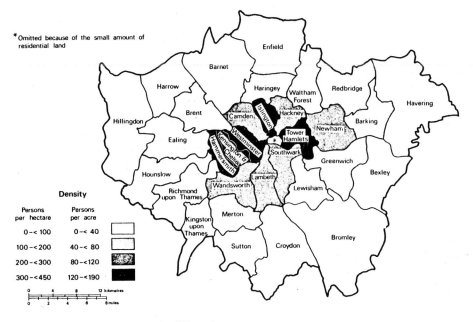

Source: GLC, *London Facts and Figures*, London, 1973.

- A shift from local authority schools to church schools;

- Aging of the population in recent housing districts and in the redevelopment areas of the fifties and sixties.

Figure 2. Live Births in London 1965-1978

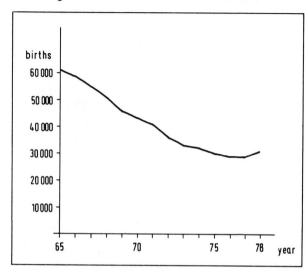

Source: Greater London Council, Research and Statistics Group, "Live Births 1965-1978", London, 1979.

Figure 3. Actual and Projected School Enrolments in London, 1965-1990

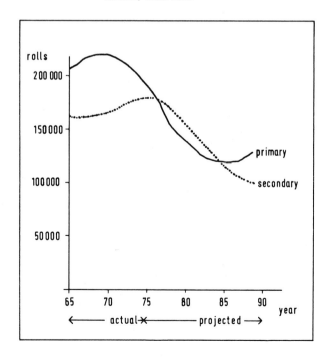

Source: Greater London Council, Research and Statistics Group, "Past and Projected Divisional Rolls Split by Sex and Age Group", London, 24 January 1980.

Some schools have suffered a drop in enrolments of 30 percent or more within five years, especially in socially deprived areas. ILEA has been helping these schools to keep most of their teaching staff despite the decreasing number of pupils ("staff allowance") and to pay staff for office work, library work and supervising children on their way to places where they can enjoy games, outdoor sports and swimming.

Assessing the Extent of the Surplus

As a local education authority considered to be educationally and administratively progressive, and because of its location in the capital, ILEA's activities have always been under particularly critical review by the public. This led the Greater London Council (GLC) to review all its thousands of properties in terms of utilisation rates, structural qualities and other factors. As a follow-up, the ILEA has started to keep an "Accommodation Register" covering data on all premises used for educational activities, room by room, with information about size, environmental qualities, current use, potential use, etc. The data will be computerised to facilitate retrieval of information on surplus or on necessary reorganisations and may also be used to simulate effects of alternative redeployment policies.

Using Surplus Space

A great number of examples of reuse can be found in London. The type of reuse, though, is specific to metropolitan environments or inner city situations. In urban areas, like London, space is not needed for community services to the same extent as in other surroundings, since these services, e.g. meeting places and social facilities, can be found anywhere in the inner city.

The types of reuse listed below can therefore be regarded as being specific to London or similar metropolitan communities:

Teachers' Centres, Learning Materials Service, Educational Television Centre

When school buildings became surplus, they were first used as central service facilities within the educational system. The first school building, put out of normal educational use in the

1960s, was remodelled to form the production and administrative centre of London Education Television. Others followed to provide centres for the production of learning materials, for in-service training of teachers, for curriculum development and for social activities (see the two examples: Educational Television Centre, Learning Material Service described at the end of this case study).

Church Schools

Like other urban areas in England, London is experiencing an increasing proportion of children in church schools while at the same time the total number of pupils is decreasing. These church schools are often housed in buildings unsuited to modern educational needs. Surplus schools in a reasonable state of repair are therefore sometimes handed over to the church. The ILEA remains responsible for the maintenance of these school buildings and covers 80 per cent of the total running costs.

Adult Education Centres and Youth Centres

Such centres have often been accommodated in schools with some surplus classrooms. As more space is released, these services take over further parts of the building. This type of reuse also presents an opportunity to introduce dual use, i.e. the centres use the remaining school spaces in late afternoon or evening hours and/or during week-ends and holidays.

Nursery Schools

Wherever possible, preferably in relation to primary schools, nursery schools are accommodated on the ground floor of existing school buildings. In 3- or 4-decker primary schools this may create problems, since the ground floor is regarded by all users as the most valuable space, offering as it does easy access and a direct relation to outdoor-activity areas. In some cases, the ILEA has even had to extend the ground floor of school buildings with surplus space on the upper floors.

Community Workshops

Although a number of community needs do not arise to the same extent in metropolitan areas as in others, people nevertheless tend to ask for spaces suitable for physical and, at the same time, productive activities. At present, the demand seems to focus on car maintenance and on constructing or maintaining sports equipment (e.g. boats). The Education Authority tries to facilitate these leisure activities by establishing community work-shops in available ground floor areas of school buildings.

Education Shops

Groups inside and outside the ILEA have proposed a network of citizen information shops at neighbourhood level. The idea is to bring educational and related opportunities closer to the residents. Surplus ground floor spaces of well-located schools could be used for some of the proposed "shops" and the network could be further extended by using former shops and work-shops with easy access. With a growing surplus of school accommodation and a developing interest in adult and recurrent education ILEA hopes to find political backing for the education shops idea.

Students Housing

Upper floors of Victorian school buildings tend to become surplus first. Access and location within the building make these spaces unattractive for many educational and community uses. ILEA has therefore proposed to use these spaces for student accommodation or for housing the homeless. The authority recognizes the fact that this may mean considerable investments to provide separate access, bathroom and kitchen facilities, etc.

Small Factories, Offices and Workshops

As more school buildings become available in the future, ILEA intends to rent or sell buildings in order to attract small businesses to areas in the city centre. However, in some instances ILEA has had difficulties in selling surplus school buildings that were not needed for other public services. The reason was that most of these buildings were located on sites that nobody really wanted and/or that the buildings were "listed", i.e. are historical buildings — often in a bad state of repair — which cannot be destroyed.

Using surplus accommodation in existing school buildings for additional purposes usually creates less problems than redeploying a whole school. In London a move to close a school often clashes with "parental choice"— especially since many old school buildings house old and established schools. This means that schools cannot be declared surplus on the basis of rational considerations only: sometimes a school building has to be kept for emotional reasons even if rationally it ought to be given up. Consequently it is extremely difficult to coordinate supply and demand in an effective way and to create schools of a size which allows a sufficient variety of courses and the economic use of buildings. A typical example of the kind of difficulties encountered by the local authority is that of an underused school in Paddington which as a result of local pressures, public enquiries and a press campaign had to be kept open.

ILEA does not redeploy its own surplus only. It also makes use of empty school buildings outside London. In recent years, it has established several outdoor education centres in attractive surroundings, i.e. in the South-West of England and in Wales. Some of these are particularly suited for field studies in disciplines such as biology or geography.

Future Prospects

On the basis of current forecasts about pupil rolls and expected building programmes, ILEA has calculated that, in the late eighties, all pupils could in theory be accommodated in post World War II buildings. This does not, however, seem to be a realistic proposition: parental choice is linked to the reputation of the older schools and their better location generally recognised. In addition, old schools — despite certain deficiencies — often provide a more satisfactory environment than the newer ones and pupils, teachers and parents like them because of their "character".

Heavy depopulation as a result of suburbanisation and new town policies coupled with urban blight has led the authorities to revise their policies with a view to revitalising Inner London. As a consequence the ILEA forecasts local increases in the school population, especially in new housing development areas. Since there is a long-standing tradition of corporate planning in London involving all public agencies concerned, ILEA is taking part also in the planning of new housing schemes.

A major programme for the 1980s is to revitalise the London Docklands. The overall objective is to seize the opportunity of large parts of the Docklands becoming available for development to remedy housing, social, environmental, employment and communication deficiencies. Close cooperation between different agencies has led to a very sensible approach in terms of educational provision. Because of a declining population in the past, most schools in the area now have spare capacity. By carefully locating and phasing housing developments in relation to the existing schools, there will be no need for new schools to be built in the area. Instead, existing schools will be brought up to current standards by adding playing fields, halls, gymnasia and swimming pools, and making provision for community use (Figure 4).

Figure 4. Existing Primary and Secondary Schools and Other Education Establishments in the Area Covered by London Docklands Strategic Plan

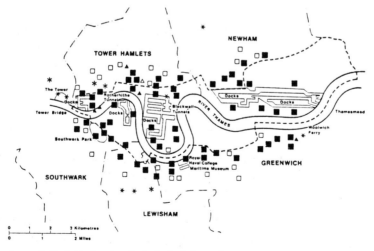

Source: Docklands Joint Committee, *London Docklands Strategic Plan*, London, 1976.

LEARNING MATERIALS SERVICE
Highbury Station Road
London N 1

Formerly: LONDON EDUCATIONAL
    TELEVISION CENTRE (1965-70)
    LAYCOCK SCHOOL (pre-1965)

Built: approx. 1900
Redeployed: 1971 (new entrance hall, partitions,
    redecoration)
Total floor area: approx. 1 500 m² (3 storeys,
    2 mezzanine floors)

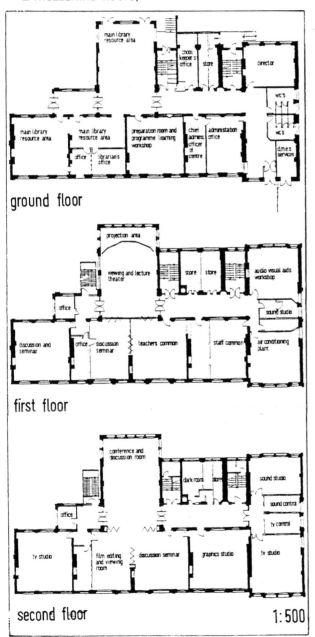

ground floor

first floor

second floor   1:500

Source: Greater London Council Department of Architecture and Civic Design, "Multi-media
Teachers' Centre at Laycock Building Highbury", London 1970

Laycock School was the first school in London to become fully available for alternative use. Between 1965 and 1970 it provisionally served as London Educational Television Centre. It was afterwards remodelled to house the Learning Materials Service for all Inner London schools.

The school was remodelled on a very tight budget which only allowed the building of a new entrance hall, altering some partitions and redecorating the interior. It was not possible to improve the external appearance.

The ground floor includes offices, a generous library, a well-equipped programme learning workshop and stores for learning materials ready to be handed out to Inner London schools.

The first floor includes discussion and seminar rooms for teachers, an audio-visual aids workshop, a viewing and lecture theatre, the staff room, more storage rooms and a teachers common room where teachers can meet, formally and informally.

The second floor contains conference and discussion rooms, television- and sound-studios with associated control rooms, a graphics studio and a viewing room.

The Learning Materials Service encourages teachers to contribute to the development of work in the London schools. Technical staff help in the design and production of learning materials in the form of booklets, films, sound or television tapes. Teachers wishing to receive ideas or aids for their teaching can also come to the centre to get information and materials. The centre also promotes valuable informal contacts among teachers of London schools. At present, teachers in London are especially interested in exchanging their experiences and problems concerning multi-cultural education, community involvement in school activities and staffing conditions in a situation of decreasing enrolments.

Easily accessible to teachers

The audio-visual aids workshop

The graphics department

106

EDUCATIONAL TELEVISION CENTRE

Thackeray Road
London SW8

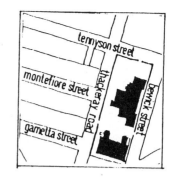

Formerly: TENNYSON SECONDARY SCHOOL

Built: 1899
Redeployed: 1970 (roof repairs, re-wiring, air conditioning, strengthening of floors, flooring, lighting, painting, furniture and fittings)
Total floor area: studio block approx. 2 000 m² (4 storeys, 2 mezzanine floors), administration building approx. 1 200 m² (3 storeys, 2 mezzanine floors)

The Educational Television Centre was first housed in Laycock School (1965-70), the first school building to be put out of normal school use in London after World War II. The Centre was then moved to Tennyson Secondary School which was remodelled to serve the specific needs of the Centre.

Of the two buildings of Tennyson School one is used for the administration and the other constitutes the studio block.

The studio block includes garages for mobile production studios on the ground floor as well as workshops, a sound studio, tape stores and the ventilation plants. The first and second floors accommodate changing rooms, a training studio, rehearsal rooms and two production studios with control rooms. The top floor is reserved for workshops and for storing stage properties.

As the centre of production, the studio block has been remodelled mainly with regard to technical requirements. This includes strengthening of floors, blocking of windows, introducing acoustical elements and a ventilation system. It was not possible, however, to make any major changes in the external or internal appearance of the building. In contrast, the administration block was remodelled with a view to providing an attractive working environment. This building includes a canteen served by a well-equipped kitchen, offices, a cutting room, a projection room, and the graphics department adjacent to a roof garden.

Educational Television Centre is the home of London Educational Television which serves all London schools with several daily cable programmes as well as taped programmes handed out to individual schools on request. By issuing frequent bulletins, the Educational Television Centre seeks to make its facilities and programmes widely known.

The outer appearance does not reveal the highly technical contents

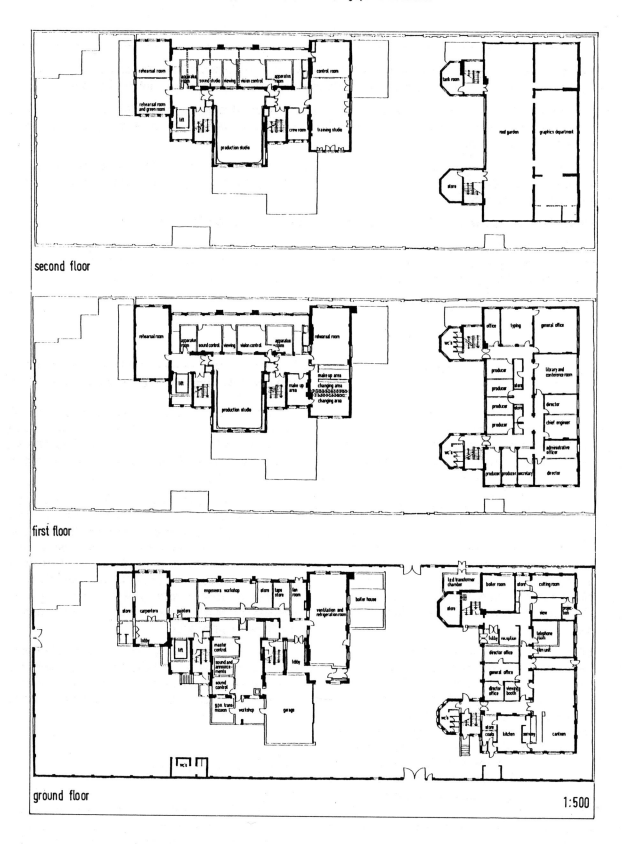

second floor

first floor

ground floor

1:500

Source: Greater London Council Department of Architecture and Civic Design, "Tennyson Secondary School Battersea – Adaptations for Television Relay Centre", London 1967.

Identity: Coventry, 340 000 inhabitants (1977), one of the centres of the British car and bicycle manufacturing industry, is located in the Midlands approximately 150 km north of London.

Main reasons for surplus space: Aging population in new housing areas, decline in births, new purpose-built comprehensive schools replacing old secondary schools, the latter being adapted to replace old primary school premises.

Quantity of surplus space: About 30 per cent capacity in terms of pupil places. Only a few schools have been closed, the rest of the surplus is used to improve standards of educational provision and to introduce social facilities.

Authorities concerned: The City of Coventry, and its Education Department.

Most important points: Special attention given to areas of educational and social disadvantage, surplus used to improve existing facilities, remove temporary accommodation units and satisfy other educational needs, e.g. by creating community education centres and teachers' centres.

Context and Main Reasons for Surplus Space

Coventry is an important manufacturing town in the South Midlands. Following the complete destruction of the city centre during World War II, the city experienced an extensive period of redevelopment with a great number of new housing schemes to cater for a rapidly growing population.

In 1950 the City of Coventry took an early decision to depart from a tiered system of secondary education, and to build new comprehensive schools at the periphery. In 1974 the secondary school system of the city became fully comprehensive.

Extensive building programmes for new comprehensive schools resulted in surplus school accommodation much earlier than elsewhere: even in times of increasing enrolments Coventry had surplus school spaces. With falling birth rates in recent years, the amount of surplus has increased further. In 1978 alone, four primary schools, a child guidance clinic (an institution designed to help children who suffer from behavioural problems without being mentally or physically ill) and various classrooms in another two schools became available. The city expects more surplus in future years.

Primary schools are among the most affected for two reasons. They are the first institutions to feel the effects of falling birth rates. In addition, Coventry's policy to replace old secondary schools by new comprehensive schools and to turn many of the redundant secondary schools into primary schools has automatically increased the number of surplus primary schools.

The first comprehensive schools built were very large since they were planned for a 12-form entry. Today, this size of school is no longer regarded as viable for educational reasons. The City of Coventry has therefore decided to admit reduced numbers of children to these large comprehensive schools: an 8-form entry has become usual. The ensuing surplus has mainly been used to improve the level of provision.

Finally, the aging population in the rapidly developed housing districts of the fifties and sixties has also made redundant a certain amount of primary school and, subsequently, secondary school accommodation.

Using Surplus Space

The date of construction, together with an analysis of the structural and spatial qualities of a building, makes it possible to determine to what extent it is substandard. As surplus arises and resources become available, substandard schools are remodelled. The first concern is always to upgrade these buildings to meet modern educational requirements. Improving educational standards may mean providing 20 to 50 per cent more floor area per pupil. If surplus is available beyond this mark, it is used for community purposes (see the example of Hearsall Community Primary School, described at the end of this case study. For the building year 1979/1980 Coventry invested £483 200 on improvement projects compared to £200 500 spent on "basic need projects" — i.e. on new school building construction).

Surplus also allows temporary accommodation units to be removed. Units which cannot be moved economically are demolished, other units are transferred to sites where there is an urgent need for additional accommodation for a limited period only.

As well as meeting the needs of the established educational system, the Education Service seeks also to satisfy other educational needs:

Nursery schools/pre-schools

Nursery schools and pre-schools are a rather recent feature of public education in Coventry (as in other parts of England). Nursery schools usually house 4-6 playgroups which are often supervised with parent involvement. These schools are preferably introduced in available ground floor areas of empty schools or of partly empty primary schools (see the example of Southfields Community Education Centre described at the end of this case study).

Community Education Centres

Community Education Centres provide facilities for adult education, minority group teaching, club and informal group meetings and many other activities. They are maintained both by the Local Authority and Charities. Community Education Centres in Coventry tend to use upper floors of old school buildings since these are not regarded as suitable for nursery and primary education (cf. Southfields Community Education Centre).

Teachers' Centres

Teachers' Centres constitute focal points for curriculum development and in-service training of teachers and offer facilities for all members of the education service to meet formally as well as informally. In 1972 Coventry remodelled an old school building to become one of the first Teachers' Centres. This has received national recognition (see the example of Elm Bank Teachers' Centre described at the end of this case study).

Beyond these types of reuse for education in its widest sense, the Education Department intends to introduce more community facilities, as additional surplus space becomes available. From the viewpoint of the Department, the following purposes should be given priority:

— Meeting places for old people;

— Youth centres;

— Career service agencies;

— Workshops for production by pupils;

— Workshops to offer training courses and temporary job opportunities for school leavers who have been unable to find permanent employment.

Possible uses will be the subject of discussion between the Education Department, other departments of the City of Coventry and other public agencies interested in reusing surplus school space.

New Policies

Until now the Education Department of the City of Coventry has always made use of available spaces for educational purposes. This has allowed a number of improvements to be made: first, the introduction of comprehensive education, already mentioned; second, standards of educational provision well above national average, both in terms of space standards and facilities offered; and, finally, provision for other forms of education.

The educational needs satisfied in Coventry are extensive. But they comply with the overall educational policies of Coventry and reflect a general strategy to retain a maximum of the school building stock in the educational service. This strategy is based on the assumption that birth rates will rise again from the mid-eighties, which would mean increasing demands for school spaces from 1990.

With decreasing funds available for education, the Education Department seeks to focus its activities on "areas of educational and social disadvantage". In Conventry these are identified by the following factors:

a) Socio-economic group of head of household;
b) Lack of basic amenity (i.e. bath, hot water supply, inside WC);
c) Overcrowding, (i.e. more than one person per room);
d) Number of children in receipt of free school meals;
e) One-parent families;
f) Absenteeism;
g) Number of pupils with fathers of overseas origin;
h) Pupil turnover;
i) Take-up of special school places (excluding those for physically handicapped pupils);
k) Households without a car;
l) Unemployment;
m) Results of primary school reading survey.

Accordingly, the number of pupils residing in areas of educational and social disadvantage was in January 1977:

Primary schools:	15 858 (42.7%)
Secondary schools:	7 976 (27.6%)
Total	23 834 (36.1%)

Investigations into schools in these areas have revealed the need for additional improvements in the educational sector. Overall surplus will help to raise standards of provision.

The Education Department has however now reached the stage where it can foresee that the demands for spare accommodation from the education service will soon be satisfied. It therefore intends to involve other public authorities in an attempt to satisfy non-educational needs as more school spaces become available.

HEARSALL COMMUNITY PRIMARY SCHOOL

Bristol Road, Earlsdon
Coventry

Formerly: HEARSALL PRIMARY SCHOOL

Built: approx. 1910
Redeployed: 1970 (carpeting, decorating, furniture and fittings, staircase, lighting)
Total floor area: approx. 2 000 m² (2/3 storeys)

Hearsall Community Primary School is being remodelled on an open-plan basis. It will provide 10 home bases, each for about 30 children. In addition to each base, there will be a variety of practical areas where children can work, mixing freely with children from other bases.

The school building will house a nursery school, an infants' school, a junior school and community facilities.

Particular care is given to improving access, divorcing pedestrian routes from vehicular service routes and providing fire escapes, and to rendering the site more attractive.

On a total budget of £40 000, the following improvements will be made:

1.   All fittings will be changed to suit children of junior age.

2.   Except for wet practical areas and areas surrounding the cloak accommodation, all teaching spaces will have carpeted floors. The wet practical areas will have tiled floors. The area surrounding the cloaks provision in each home base will have heavy-duty-sheet venyle flooring.

3.   All wall services except below worktops will be covered with pin-up boarding from a height of 2 ft. to a height of 6 ft.

4.   Each home base will be provided with a storage space suitable for storing classroom equipment and materials.

5.   Lavatories are refitted and divided into a girls- and a boys-section.

6.   An attractive main entrance will be created both for children and the community.

7.   The present hall will be provided with facilities for storing physical education equipment and a portable stage.

8.   Outside, a large sandpit with a portable cover will be created. A grassed area will be provided and a small garden space will be made around an existing tree in the playground.

9.   On the ground floor, rooms will be combined to form a parents' medical inspection room.

Improving educational facilities at minimum cost...

without sacrificing historic details

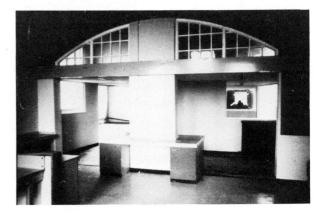

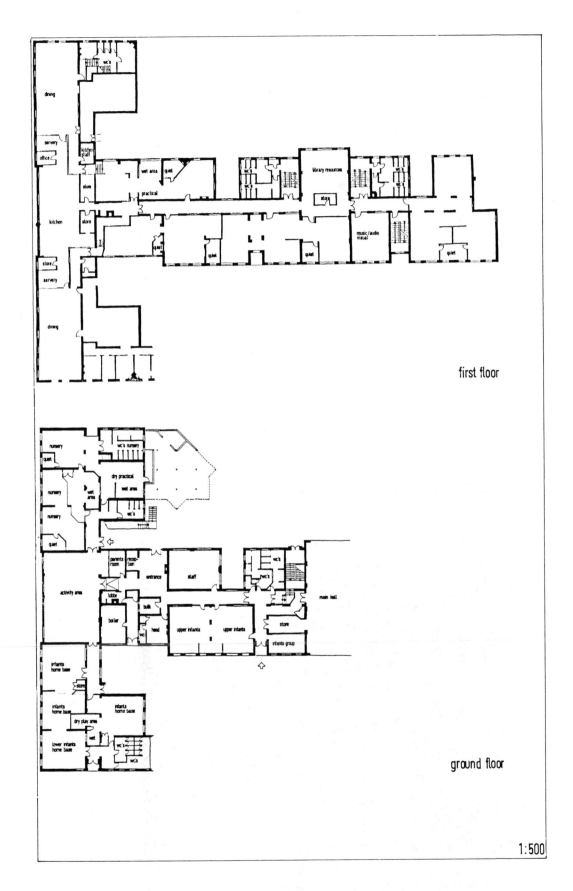

first floor

ground floor

1:500

Source: City of Coventry, City Architect and Planning Officer, "Hearsall J.M.I.", Coventry 1978.

SOUTHFIELDS COMMUNITY EDUCATION CENTRE

Gulson Road
Coventry

Formerly: SOUTHFIELDS PRIMARY SCHOOL

Built: 1900
Remodelled: 1978 (new entrance hall, lighting, furniture, fittings, floorings, staircase)
Total floor area: approx. 1 500 m² (2 storeys)

In 1975 Southfields Primary School moved into new buildings adjacent to the old school building which has been remodelled to form a community education centre. Temporary accommodation and former extensions of the old building were removed, but it was not possible to improve the external appearance further. It seemed to be more important to concentrate on the interior providing good educational and social facilities.

On the upper floor, facilities include a lounge for informal meetings, a public library, a kitchen for the public to make coffee or tea, and other facilities which encourage informal contacts among people from the neighbourhood.

The upper floor also provides meeting rooms and classrooms for teaching immigrants.

The ground floor includes nursery school classes, each containing a play area with carpeted and wooden floors, a wet area with built-in sinks and worktops, a storage area and WC's/washrooms. A monitoring room allows teachers and parents to watch children at work.

The Community Education Centre is jointly financed by the Local Education Authority and by Charities.

On the first floor: the community education centre

On the ground floor: the nursery school

ELM BANK TEACHERS' CENTRE

Mile Lane
Coventry

Formerly: CHEYLESMORE SECONDARY
   MODERN SCHOOL

Built: 1911
Redeployed: 1972-74 (new main entrance, lighting, furniture, fittings, carpets)
Total floor area: approx. 2 500 m² (2 storeys)

The new entrance

The publication department

The reference library

A meeting room

Elm Bank Teachers' Centre is a spacious, extensively remodelled former secondary school situated conveniently for the whole city and possessing a large car park.

The upper floor includes photographic and reprographic rooms, an audio-visual laboratory, television and recording units, a resources library, general workshop areas, bases for local projects, several discussion areas and a large meeting hall.

On the ground floor, social facilities include a dining/coffee lounge served by a well-equipped kitchen, a bar lounge and other amenities which encourage valuable informal contacts among members from different sections of the education service, and provide refreshments for teachers attending courses, meetings and conferences.

Coventry has maintained a teachers' centre since 1960. The success of a provisionally housed first centre encouraged the Education Authority to extend this type of provision. Elm Bank encourages teachers to contribute to their own development and to the development of the work in schools and colleges. Staff offers support to working parties, study groups and courses, and collects the results and resources for subsequent dissemination. By means of frequent bulletins to schools and a variety of exhibitions of local and national projects as well as commercial materials, the Centre seeks to encourage a wider awareness of educational developments.

The management, education and social committees of the Centre include teachers, advisers and administrators. The Centre acts as a focal point for in-service training and curriculum development.

It was not possible to make any major changes in the external appearance of the building, and it was decided therefore to concentrate on providing good educational and social areas with an attractive and welcoming "non-school" atmosphere. Attention was also paid to the quality of furniture and fittings, which together with the carpeting of the whole building, adds an air of luxury to many areas.

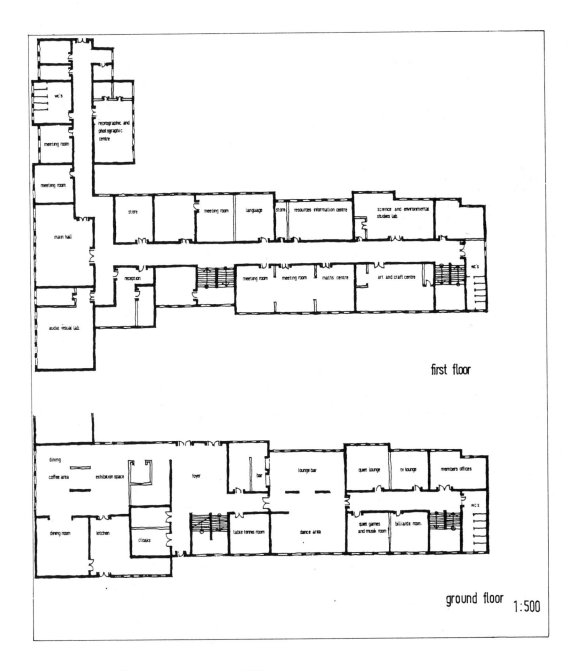

Source: City of Coventry, "Elm Bank Teachers' Centre", Coventry 1979.

Identity: Wales, a small country, with an area of 20 768 km² and a population of approximately 2.8 million, forms part of the United Kingdom. It has, however, its own distinctive history, language and culture.

Main reasons for surplus space: Depopulation of rural as well as urban areas; educational reorganisation.

Quantity of surplus space: No country-wide figures available (the fact that some 200 school buildings have been converted into outdoor pursuits centres is in itself an indication of the extent of the surplus).

Authorities concerned: Welsh Office Education Department and eight local authorities.

Most important points: Use of vacated schools as field study or outdoor pursuits centres established as satellites to existing schools; provision of community facilities in area schools as well as in surplus school buildings as part of a policy to reverse depopulation; establishment of teachers' centres and resource centres to develop the professional capacity of teachers; use of surplus to relieve a temporary pressure for places in higher and further education; variety of uses for other educational, community and private purposes.

Context and Main Reasons for Surplus Space

Wales is a mainly rural country and mostly agricultural. Heavy industries, like coal mines, slate quarries, iron and steel works, which once brought prosperity, were concentrated in the valleys of the south and in the north-east and north-west parts of the country. At the turn of the century, rapid industrialisation led to the depopulation of rural areas. This trend continued throughout this century and has only recently been halted thanks to Government and local authority initiatives to bring light industry and other types of employment back into these areas.

Wales contains, in infinite variety, large areas of natural beauty. It has three National Parks, four designated areas of outstanding beauty and 34 National Nature Reserves, which together make up for a quarter of the land area.

It has been administratively linked with England for over 400 years, with common systems of law and education and of services administered by Central Government in London. In recent years, however, more and more Central Government responsibility and control have been devolved and now reside in the Secretary of State for Wales. The system of education, a national system locally administered, although common to England and Wales, has since 1978 formed part of the Secretary of State's responsibility and is administered by the Welsh Office Education Department.

Eight local authorities administer the education service, each with a committee of elected members serviced by salaried officials. The design and provision of schools is a matter for local authorities subject to certain statutory and financial controls which are exerted by Welsh Office Education Department, which also provides information and advice on current building and educational trends. Matters of topical interest are dealt with by the publication of Design Studies.

Depopulation throughout this century has resulted in the closure of many schools. When schools were left with so few pupils (and occasionally with only one teacher) that they became educationally non-viable, the authorities invariably resorted to closure concentrating teaching in neighbouring schools. The raising of the school leaving age, the reorganisation of secondary education and ensuing curriculum reforms have also implied a restructuring of the school networks leaving a number of schools empty. Despite an initial lack of formal procedures for reuse, practices for considering possible alternative uses have gradually become established.

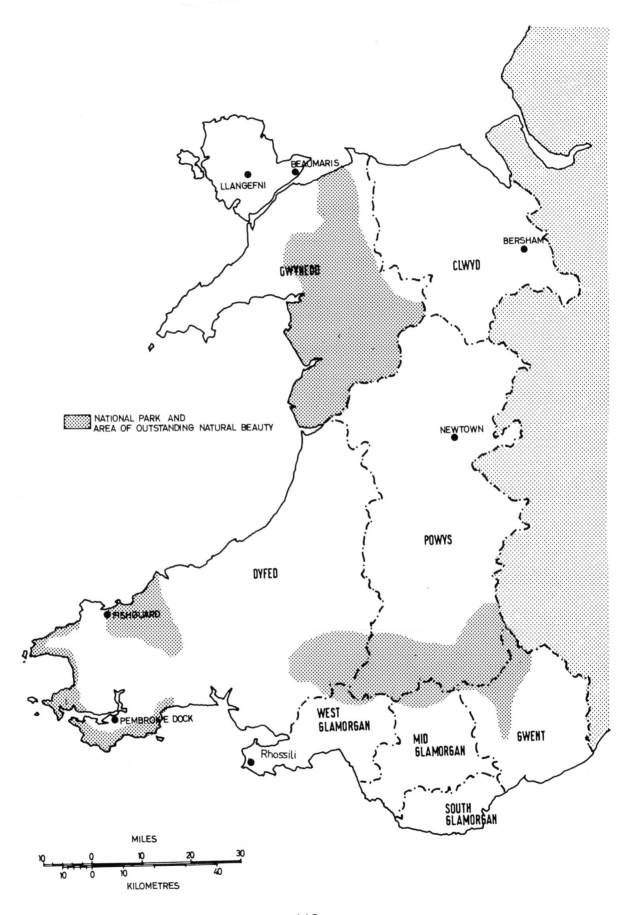

NATIONAL PARK AND
AREA OF OUTSTANDING NATURAL BEAUTY

LLANGEFNI

BEAUMARIS

GWYNEDD

CLWYD

BERSHAM

NEWTOWN

POWYS

DYFED

FISHGUARD

PEMBROKE DOCK

Rhossili

WEST
GLAMORGAN

MID
GLAMORGAN

GWENT

SOUTH
GLAMORGAN

MILES

10   0   10   20   30

10   0   10   40

KILOMETRES

Using Surplus Space

From a register of reallocated school buildings, five categories of reuse can be distinguished and the order in which local authorities have usually considered possible alternative uses is as follows: first, other needs of the educational service; secondly, the educational, social and cultural needs of the community; thirdly, the needs of other local social service agencies; fourthly, the possibility of selling the school to other interested education authorities; lastly, the sale to private individuals or to commercial enterprises. Even if needs were often examined in this order, the decisions have always depended on local circumstances.

The use made of vacated schools for alternative educational purposes plots the growth and expansion of the service as well as changes in educational practice. Thus the raising of the school leaving age in 1954 and 1972 and the accompanying expansion of curricular and extra-curricular activities are marked by the establishment of residential field-study and outdoor pursuits centres. A large number of such centres have been established by English and Welsh authorities servicing inner city, urban and suburban areas. More recently the pattern has continued with an increasing number of individual schools seeking to establish satellites, if possible within a reasonable distance in order to offer regular opportunities of extended activities, occasionally with the added bonus of residential experience. Many schools have purchased and run minibuses to enable them to take advantage of centres which are slightly more distant. The frequency of this type of use reflects the location of vacated schools, either in areas of natural beauty and resources or where the terrain offers opportunities for such activities as mountaineering, rock climbing, hill walking or sailing and canoeing.

In recent years there has been a greater awareness of the need to provide for the community, and in rural areas the use of vacated schools for community purposes or the establishment of "area" schools with facilities for social, cultural and leisure activities is part of a policy to reverse the migration trend and to enrich the quality of life in often very isolated areas. It is interesting to note the success of the area school[1]. Community facilities have been heavily used and quite a few pupils have been attracted to the school from outside the catchment area. Before handing over a vacated school for community use some authorities ensure that it is in a reasonable state of repair and decoration. The variety of spaces available in vacated schools and the heating and servicing arrangements meet the needs of the community better than the traditional meeting places, often badly or expensively heated, such as church and chapel vestries.

The development of in-service training of teachers produced the need for a network of "Teachers' Centres" and the increased reliance on resource material and audio-visual aids, which often needs to be produced locally, has resulted in the establishment of resource centres. There are numerous examples of both types of centre being established in former schools.

The availability of surplus school accommodation conveniently located and of reasonable quality is a fairly recent phenomenon in urban areas. It is the result of:

— Changes in the age profile of established communities;

— Natural population movements or enforced movements as in the case of slum clearance schemes or new housing developments;

— A marked decline in birth rates.

Such surplus has often been seen as an opportunity for meeting what is recognised as a temporary pressure for places in higher and further education, or for providing facilities for sectors of the education service which had previously often been neglected because of lack of funds, such as youth clubs and centres for adult education.

The Welsh case studies, chosen at random but drawn from most parts of the country, provide examples of several different types of reuse:

— Rhossili Outdoor Pursuits Centre, West Glamorgan;

— Beaumaris Outdoor Activities and Community Centres, Gwynedd;

— Llangefni Teachers' Centre, Gwynedd;

— Newtown Technical College, Powys;

— Fishguard Youth Centre and Pembroke Dock Further Education Centre, Dyfed;

— Bersham Museum and Study Centre, Clwyd.

RHOSSILI OUTDOOR PURSUITS CENTRE, WEST GLAMORGAN

The centre is situated at the south-west tip of the Gower peninsula, an area of natural beauty and rich in interest for outdoor activities and field studies. Much of the adjoining land is National Trust property. The sea cliffs near Rhossili provide a variety of rock climbing areas, the open moorland behind is ideal for the introduction of orienteering and for pony trekking, while the sea provides safe areas for canoe surfing.

The centre was established on the closure, in 1970, of the small local primary school, which was replaced by a school in the nearby village of Knelston. It has been suggested that part of the original building may have been a 17th century "workhouse", i.e. an institution for the poor. The authority initially undertook minimal and low-cost structural modifications and alterations to the original building to enable small groups of children and their teachers to be accommodated in a somewhat spartan manner and on a self-catering basis. However, in 1976 the centre was extended and now boasts a kitchen, washroom, showers, indoor toilets, staff sleeping-quarters, office, quiet area/library, equipment stores and a teaching area. Central heating was installed, the kitchen was properly equipped and car parking was provided in the centre grounds. It now has a permanent teaching staff and caters for groups of up to 24 children with two accompanying teachers. In the main, the courses, of an introductory nature, are run from Monday to Friday, though a few specialist courses are arranged for award schemes in activities like canoeing and rock climbing. Groups are drawn from West Glamorgan comprehensive schools.

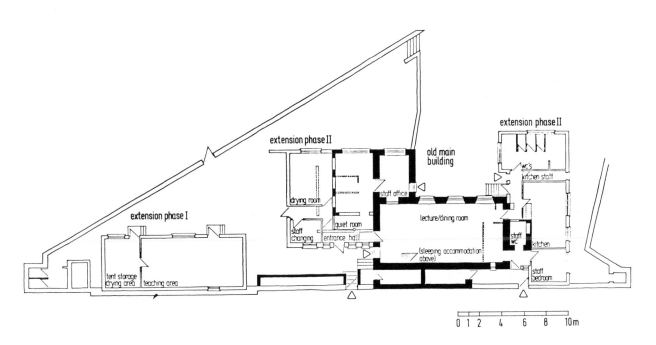

Source: West Glamorgan County Council, County Architect's Department "Rhossili Education Centre", Swansea 1975.

BEAUMARIS OUTDOOR ACTIVITIES AND COMMUNITY CENTRES, GWYNEDD

Beaumaris, a picturesque small town on the eastern shores of Anglesey with some 2 000 inhabitants, grew around a 13th century castle built by Edward I as part of a line of fortification extending along the North Wales coastal plain. Alongside this castle the David Hughes School was established in 1603 and served to give grammar school education until it was replaced in 1963 as part of the authority's secondary school reorganisation programme.

Two centres were established in the vacated premises: the community centre in part of the original school, and the outdoor activities centre in newer buildings which had served as science laboratories and dining facilities for the former school.

The community centre was provided in response to strong local pressure which resulted in saving part of a building which, because of structural problems, had been recommended for demolition. The old oak-panelled school hall now serves as an exhibition gallery and as a place for the occasional meetings of larger groups, while smaller rooms on the upper floor provide a range of committee rooms and study spaces for adult classes and for local voluntary organisations. A new library was added, establishing this site as a focal point for cultural activities in the community.

The outdoor activities centre was established to provide secondary school pupils and members of youth clubs in Gwynedd with opportunities for sailing, canoeing and hill walking along the Menai Straits in line with recommendations contained in the then recently published Newsom Report[2]. The centre provides dormitory accommodation for some 30 pupils and rooms for accompanying staff; a recreation area; a study area with small library, laboratory and workroom, including a photographic darkroom; a heated learner swimming pool, which was an addition, and boat stores and workshops. The centre is now used for two school terms by primary school pupils engaged, weekly, in environmental studies and in the third term by Gwynedd secondary school pupils following sailing and canoeing courses. At weekends it is available to youth clubs and other organisations.

It is also interesting to note that in the town of Beaumaris two 19th century schools, which were replaced as schools a long time ago, are both still in daily use: one provides housing, while the other serves as a health centre and as the local emergency fire station.

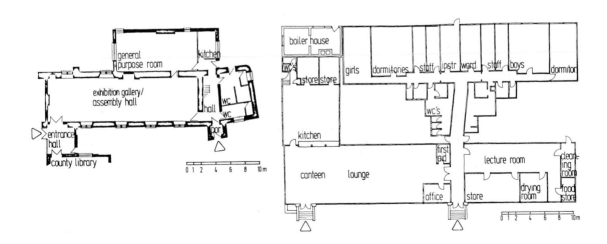

Source: Gwynedd County Council County Architect, "Beaumaris Outdoor Activity Centre", Llangefni 1975.

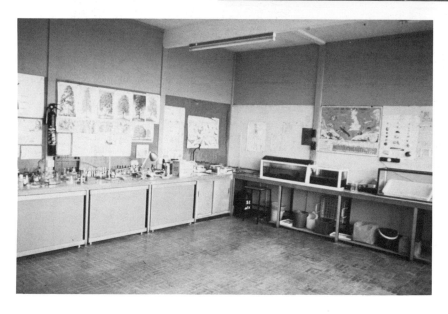

LLANGEFNI TEACHERS' CENTRE, GWYNEDD

Llangefni is a busy market town and administrative centre in the centre of Anglesey and at the hub of the road system wich serves the island. In 1970 it was decided to convert the recently replaced primary school into a Teachers' Centre. The central site and its proximity to the educational administrative offices made this a most suitable location. A number of other school facilities on the same site, of which some were temporary units, have also been reused (see site plan) and are good examples of needs surplus accommodation can help meet.

The teachers participated in planning the alterations and in remodelling and redecorating their new centre. Thus, with some £15 000 the building was imaginatively converted to provide a common room, a library, a meeting room, an exhibition area, a visual aids room, a darkroom, an office and a snacks area.

The centre is used extensively for in-service training and as a meeting place for teachers of the island. It serves also as a resource centre for island schools with an audio-visual loan service and with special library facilities for teachers.

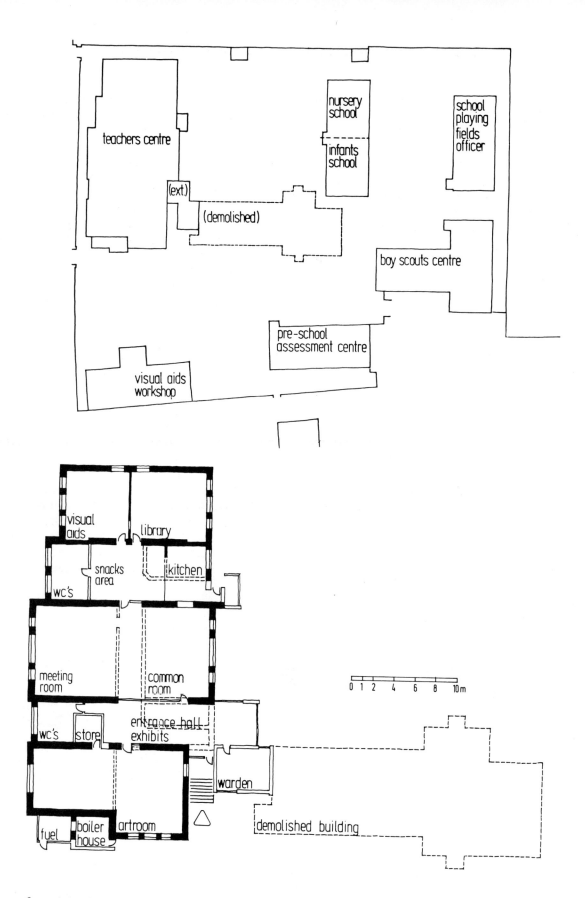

Source: Anglesey County Council County Architect, "Proposed Teachers' Centre, Llangefni", Llangefni 1968.

NEWTOWN TECHNICAL COLLEGE, POWYS

Newtown, a small market town in Mid-Wales became the subject of planned growth with the aim of doubling its population of some five and a half thousand by the early 1980s. A small technical college served the needs of the town and the surrounding rural area, offering a range of agricultural, craft apprenticeship and commercial courses. The creation of industrial training boards in the late 60s saw an expansion of further education and an urgent need for additional space at the college. The restricted college site precluded the possibility of additional large buildings and the existing permanent building surrounded by demountable huts provided only a short-term solution to the further education needs of the town. Shortage of resources suggested that it would be at least fifteen years before the college could be replaced.

Against this background, a church school built in 1827 on an adjacent site and a county primary school built in 1874 and situated across the road from the college were replaced. Although the buildings of both schools had been declared severly substandard for primary school use and although both had structural problems, the college sought and obtained permission to renovate them, creating in one a motor vehicle workshop and in the other a base for building construction work. The work involved was undertaken by staff and students and the projects, in addition to providing much needed specialist spaces, introduced a welcome degree of realism into building courses at the college.

Kerry Road Church School: Built in 1827, was adapted for college use in 1971. The old school cruciform in plan, consisted of series of classrooms divided by wood and glass partitions. It had outside toilets and a small lean-to kitchen which was added in the post-war years. Partitions were removed in the main area and the wooden floor was replaced by a concrete one with a vehicle inspection pit sufficiently large for instruction and for group activity. One side of the building was opened up to allow vehicular access. The small kitchen area was converted to form a "stores" area and a small side room was turned into an electrical projects area.

New Road Junior School: Built in 1874 and adapted for college use in 1969, it was subsequently modified to provide additional project experience for students in the building construction department. Early remodelling work provided workshops for woodwork, plumbing, masonry and other construction work. The height of the original building allows the construction of two-storey houses within it. In recent years, facilities for painting and decorating have been incorporated and extensions have provided storage space and covered outdoor workshop areas.

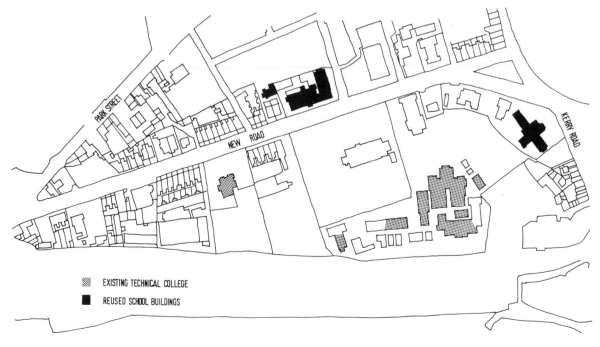

░░ EXISTING TECHNICAL COLLEGE

■ REUSED SCHOOL BUILDINGS

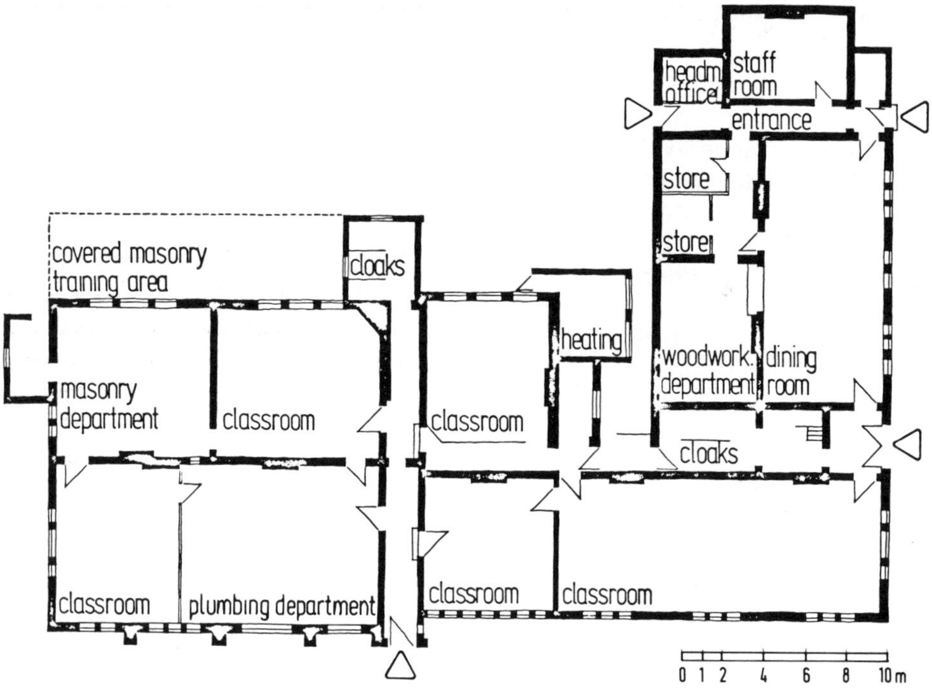

headm office
staff room
entrance
store
store
covered masonry training area
cloaks
heating
woodwork department
dining room
masonry department
classroom
classroom
cloaks
classroom
plumbing department
classroom
classroom
0 1 2 4 6 8 10m

Source: Montgomery Education Authority, "New Road School Newtown – Proposed Conversion of Infants Block".

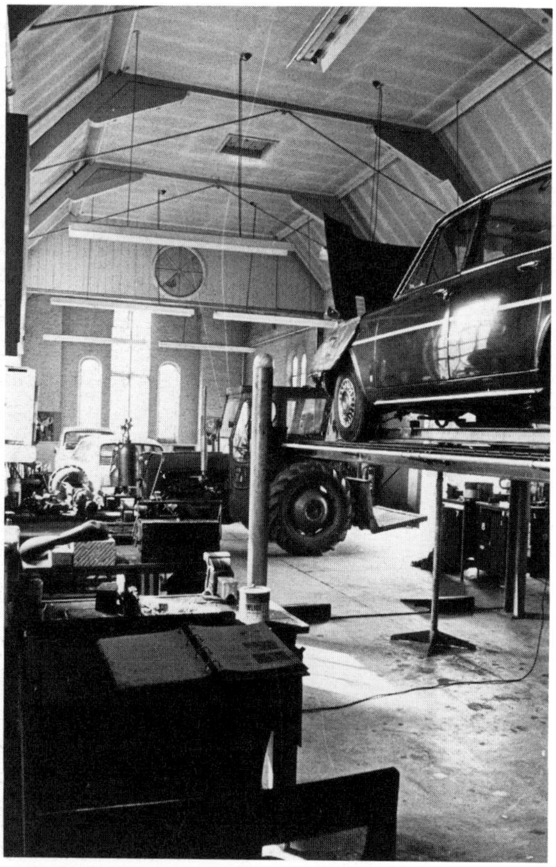

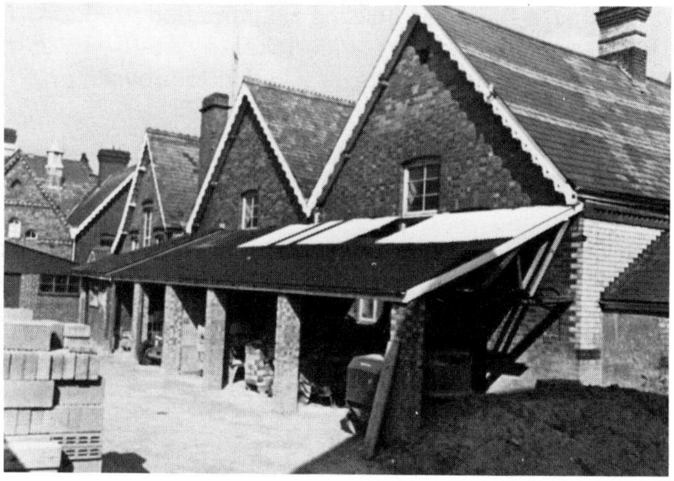

FURTHER EDUCATION AND YOUTH CENTRES, FISHGUARD AND PEMBROKE DOCK, DYFED

In 1960 the former Pembrokeshire Education Committee approved and initiated a ten-year building programme designed to provide a fulltime youth service, available to young people aged between 14 and 21 in the urban areas of the county. As part of this programme it identified a number of school premises which would be surplus to requirements. Fishguard and Pembroke Dock were two such schools.

Fishguard: A busy ferry terminal, with regular sailings for Ireland, has a population of some 5 000 inhabitants. This is an interesting example of conversion of an old grammar school, built in 1902 for 130 pupils, and remodelled in 1969 at a cost of £20 000 to provide accommodation more appropriate to the needs of teenagers and their activities. The centre, although designed for use by young people between the ages of 14 and 21 on six evenings in the week, makes the facilities freely available to various community groups and voluntary bodies. The centre is a base for subaqua work and is equipped with a compressor which is available to all subaqua groups in the county.

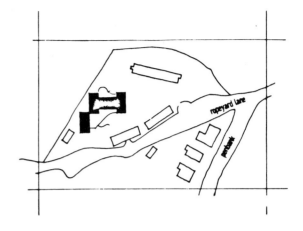

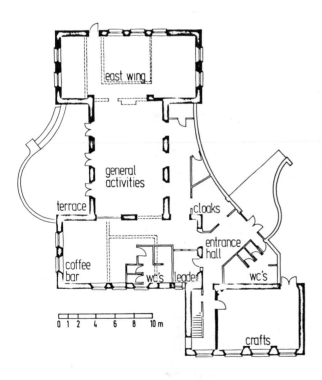

Source: Pembrokeshire Education Committee, County Architect, "Proposed Youth Centre Fishguard — Conversion of Old Grammar School", Haverfordwest 1969.

Pembroke Dock: With a population of 9 000 has suffered considerably in the last 50 years because of economic decline following the closure of the Royal Naval Dockyard. It has experienced intermittent periods of boom with the revival of defence work during the war years and the building of oil refineries and a power station, but these have not lasted. The area is one of social and economic deprivation.

The adult centre was established in 1973, in the premises of the 1902 Dockyard School, established by the Admiralty and the Church to train some 900 pupils for naval careers; from 1926 it served as an elementary school for boys, from 1944 as a mixed school and from the early 50s as the junior section of a secondary modern school. Minimal alterations, at a cost of £10 000 were undertaken mainly by a Direct Labour Force to adapt the school to adult use. The major change involved the conversion of two classrooms alongside the central hall to provide an open-plan coffee-bar lounge area which is a focal point for centre activities and an inviting social area. Workshops for pottery and for fibreglass work were developed out of old bicycle sheds. Changing rooms were converted into small seminar rooms. Otherwise the fabric of the building has not been altered.

BERSHAM MUSEUM AND STUDIES CENTRE, CLWYD

Bersham School is located in Clywedog Valley, three miles from Wrexham, which during the second half of the 18th century was a flourishing centre for ironmaking; the school was built in 1872 and was closed in 1961 but served for a while as base for physically handicapped. In 1980, it was converted into a museum and studies centre.

Some of the works were undertaken as part of a Job Creation Scheme and only involved cost of materials. Other, more specialised works were entrusted to contractors and were paid for via grants from Central Government and the local authority. At the time of writing, no accurate breakdown of costs had yet been made but the expectation was that the conversion would be made at about 30 per cent of the cost of a new museum building.

Work carried out included external improvements (like a new road, car park, tree planting, footpaths, gates, drainage), internal alterations (filling of door openings, electrical installation, electrical heating, redecoration), and minor extensions (toilet block and refreshment room).

Starting from this building, an industrial museum trail is being set up extending for eight miles consisting of: lead mines, quarries, iron works, a blacksmith forge, wrought iron works, an agricultural display, brick- and terracotta-works, corn- and paper-mills.

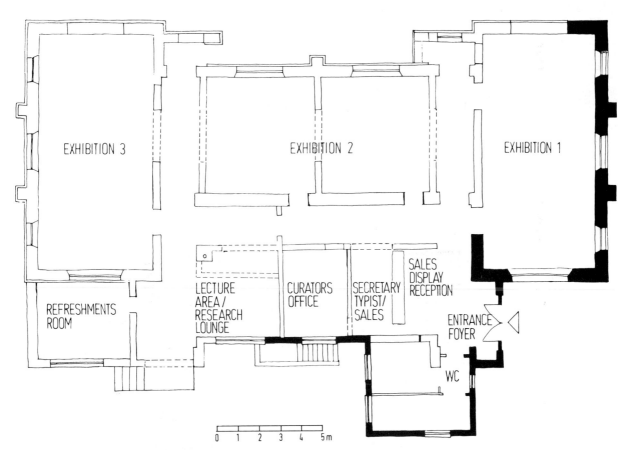

Source: Clwyd County, County Architect, "Bersham Museum – Proposed Plans", Mold 1979.

NOTES

1. "Ysgol Y Dderi. An Area School in Dyfed", *Design Study 2*, Welsh Office of Education, September 1976.

2. Newsom, *Half our Future*, A Report of the Central Advisory Council for Education, 1963.

OECD SALES AGENTS
DÉPOSITAIRES DES PUBLICATIONS DE L'OCDE

ARGENTINA – ARGENTINE
Carlos Hirsch S.R.L., Florida 165, 4° Piso (Galería Guemes)
1333 BUENOS AIRES, Tel. 33.1787.2391 y 30.7122

AUSTRALIA – AUSTRALIE
Australia and New Zealand Book Company Pty, Ltd.,
10 Aquatic Drive, Frenchs Forest, N.S.W. 2086
P.O. Box 459, BROOKVALE, N.S.W. 2100. Tel. (02) 452.44.11

AUSTRIA – AUTRICHE
OECD Publications and Information Center
4 Simrockstrasse 5300 Bonn (Germany). Tel. (0228) 21.60.45
Local Agent/Agent local :
Gerold and Co., Graben 31, WIEN 1. Tel. 52.22.35

BELGIUM – BELGIQUE
Jean De Lannoy, Service Publications OCDE
avenue du Roi 202, B-1060 BRUXELLES. Tel. 02/538.51.69

CANADA
Renouf Publishing Company Limited,
Central Distribution Centre,
61 Sparks Street (Mall),
P.O.B. 1008 - Station B,
OTTAWA, Ont. KIP 5R1.
Tel. (613)238.8985-6
Toll Free: 1-800.267.4164
Librairie Renouf Limitée
980 rue Notre-Dame,
Lachine, P.Q. H8S 2B9,
Tel. (514) 634-7088.

DENMARK – DANEMARK
Munksgaard Export and Subscription Service
35, Nørre Søgade
DK 1370 KØBENHAVN K. Tel. +45.1.12.85.70

FINLAND – FINLANDE
Akateeminen Kirjakauppa
Keskuskatu 1, 00100 HELSINKI 10. Tel. 65.11.22

FRANCE
Bureau des Publications de l'OCDE,
2 rue André-Pascal, 75775 PARIS CEDEX 16. Tel. (1) 524.81.67
Principal correspondant :
13602 AIX-EN-PROVENCE : Librairie de l'Université.
Tel. 26.18.08

GERMANY – ALLEMAGNE
OECD Publications and Information Center
4 Simrockstrasse 5300 BONN Tel. (0228) 21.60.45

GREECE – GRÈCE
Librairie Kauffmann, 28 rue du Stade,
ATHÈNES 132. Tel. 322.21.60

HONG-KONG
Government Information Services,
Publications (Sales) Office,
Beaconsfield House, 4/F.,
Queen's Road Central

ICELAND – ISLANDE
Snaebjörn Jönsson and Co., h.f.,
Hafnarstraeti 4 and 9, P.O.B. 1131, REYKJAVIK.
Tel. 13133/14281/11936

INDIA – INDE
Oxford Book and Stationery Co. :
NEW DELHI-1, Scindia House. Tel. 45896
CALCUTTA 700016, 17 Park Street. Tel. 240832

INDONESIA – INDONÉSIE
PDIN-LIPI, P.O. Box 3065/JKT., JAKARTA, Tel. 583467

IRELAND – IRLANDE
TDC Publishers – Library Suppliers
12 North Frederick Street, DUBLIN 1 Tel. 744835-749677

ITALY – ITALIE
Libreria Commissionaria Sansoni :
Via Lamarmora 45, 50121 FIRENZE. Tel. 579751/584468
Via Bartolini 29, 20155 MILANO. Tel. 365083
Sub-depositari :
Ugo Tassi
Via A. Farnese 28, 00192 ROMA. Tel. 310590
Editrice e Libreria Herder,
Piazza Montecitorio 120, 00186 ROMA. Tel. 6794628
Costantino Ercolano, Via Generale Orsini 46, 80132 NAPOLI. Tel. 405210
Libreria Hoepli, Via Hoepli 5, 20121 MILANO. Tel. 865446
Libreria Scientifica, Dott. Lucio de Biasio "Aeiou"
Via Meravigli 16, 20123 MILANO Tel. 807679
Libreria Zanichelli
Piazza Galvani 1/A, 40124 Bologna Tel. 237389
Libreria Lattes, Via Garibaldi 3, 10122 TORINO. Tel. 519274
La diffusione delle edizioni OCSE è inoltre assicurata dalle migliori librerie nelle
città più importanti.

JAPAN – JAPON
OECD Publications and Information Center,
Landic Akasaka Bldg., 2-3-4 Akasaka,
Minato-ku, TOKYO 107 Tel. 586.2016

KOREA – CORÉE
Pan Korea Book Corporation,
P.O. Box n° 101 Kwangwhamun, SÉOUL. Tel. 72.7369

LEBANON – LIBAN
Documenta Scientifica/Redico,
Edison Building, Bliss Street, P.O. Box 5641, BEIRUT.
Tel. 354429 – 344425

MALAYSIA – MALAISIE
University of Malaya Co-operative Bookshop Ltd.
P.O. Box 1127, Jalan Pantai Baru
KUALA LUMPUR. Tel. 577701/577072

THE NETHERLANDS – PAYS-BAS
Staatsuitgeverij, Verzendboekhandel,
Chr. Plantijnstraat 1 Postbus 20014
2500 EA S-GRAVENHAGE. Tel. nr. 070.789911
Voor bestellingen: Tel. 070.789208

NEW ZEALAND – NOUVELLE-ZÉLANDE
Publications Section,
Government Printing Office Bookshops:
AUCKLAND: Retail Bookshop: 25 Rutland Street,
Mail Orders: 85 Beach Road, Private Bag C.P.O.
HAMILTON: Retail: Ward Street,
Mail Orders, P.O. Box 857
WELLINGTON: Retail: Mulgrave Street (Head Office),
Cubacade World Trade Centre
Mail Orders: Private Bag
CHRISTCHURCH: Retail: 159 Hereford Street,
Mail Orders: Private Bag
DUNEDIN: Retail: Princes Street
Mail Order: P.O. Box 1104

NORWAY – NORVÈGE
J.G. TANUM A/S
P.O. Box 1177 Sentrum OSLO 1. Tel. (02) 80.12.60

PAKISTAN
Mirza Book Agency, 65 Shahrah Quaid-E-Azam, LAHORE 3.
Tel. 66839

PORTUGAL
Livraria Portugal, Rua do Carmo 70-74,
1117 LISBOA CODEX. Tel. 360582/3

SINGAPORE – SINGAPOUR
Information Publications Pte Ltd,
Pei-Fu Industrial Building,
24 New Industrial Road N° 02-06
SINGAPORE 1953, Tel. 2831786, 2831798

SPAIN – ESPAGNE
Mundi-Prensa Libros, S.A.
Castelló 37, Apartado 1223, MADRID-28001, Tel. 275.46.55
Libreria Bosch, Ronda Universidad 11, BARCELONA 7.
Tel. 317.53.08, 317.53.58

SWEDEN – SUÈDE
AB CE Fritzes Kungl Hovbokhandel,
Box 16 356, S 103 27 STH, Regeringsgatan 12,
DS STOCKHOLM. Tel. 08/23.89.00
Subscription Agency/Abonnements:
Wennergren-Williams AB,
Box 30004, S104 25 STOCKHOLM.
Tel. 08/54.12.00

SWITZERLAND – SUISSE
OECD Publications and Information Center
4 Simrockstrasse 5300 BONN (Germany). Tel. (0228) 21.60.45
Local Agents/Agents locaux
Librairie Payot, 6 rue Grenus, 1211 GENÈVE 11. Tel. 022.31.89.50

TAIWAN – FORMOSE
Good Faith Worldwide Int'l Co., Ltd.
9th floor, No. 118, Sec. 2,
Chung Hsiao E. Road
TAIPEI. Tel. 391.7396/391.7397

THAILAND – THAILANDE
Suksit Siam Co., Ltd., 1715 Rama IV Rd,
Samyan, BANGKOK 5. Tel. 2511630

TURKEY – TURQUIE
Kültur Yayinlari Is-Türk Ltd. Sti.
Atatürk Bulvari No : 191/Kat. 21
Kavaklidere/ANKARA. Tel. 17 02 66
Dolmabahce Cad. No : 29
BESIKTAS/ISTANBUL. Tel. 60 71 88

UNITED KINGDOM – ROYAUME-UNI
H.M. Stationery Office,
P.O.B. 276, LONDON SW8 5DT.
(postal orders only)
Telephone orders: (01) 622.3316, or
49 High Holborn, LONDON WC1V 6 HB (personal callers)
Branches at: EDINBURGH, BIRMINGHAM, BRISTOL,
MANCHESTER, BELFAST.

UNITED STATES OF AMERICA – ÉTATS-UNIS
OECD Publications and Information Center, Suite 1207,
1750 Pennsylvania Ave., N.W. WASHINGTON, D.C.20006 – 4582
Tel. (202) 724.1857

VENEZUELA
Libreria del Este, Avda. F. Miranda 52, Edificio Galipan,
CARACAS 106. Tel. 32.23.01/33.26.04/31.58.38

YUGOSLAVIA – YOUGOSLAVIE
Jugoslovenska Knjiga, Knez Mihajlova 2, P.O.B. 36, BEOGRAD.
Tel. 621.992

Les commandes provenant de pays où l'OCDE n'a pas encore désigné de dépositaire peuvent être adressées à :
OCDE, Bureau des Publications, 2, rue André-Pascal, 75775 PARIS CEDEX 16.
Orders and inquiries from countries where sales agents have not yet been appointed may be sent to:
OECD, Publications Office, 2, rue André-Pascal, 75775 PARIS CEDEX 16.

68656-05-1985

OECD PUBLICATIONS, 2, rue André-Pascal, 75775 PARIS CEDEX 16 - No. 43155 1985
PRINTED IN FRANCE
(95 85 01 1) ISBN 92-64-12732-1